Contents

A catalogue record for this
book is available from the
National Library of Australia

NATIONAL
LIBRARY
OF AUSTRALIA

ISBN: PB: 978-0-6454128-0-2; eBook PDF: 978-0-6454128-1-9; eBook
epub: 978-0-6454128-2-6; eBook Kindle: 978-0-6454128-3-3

Printed in Australia by Ingram Spark

Design by Lora Starling and Zara Falkiner-Rose
Illustrations by Lora Starling

Disclaimer

The material in this publication is of the nature of general comment
only and does not represent professional advice. It is not intended
to provide specific guidance for circumstances, and it should not be
relied on as the basis for any decision to take action or not take action
on any matter which it covers. Readers should obtain professional
advice where appropriate, before making any such decision. To
the maximum extent permitted by law, the author and publisher
disclaim all responsibility and liability to any person, arising directly
or indirectly from any person taking or not taking action based on the
information in this publication.

Acknowledgements

We wish to thank the following for working with author, Leslie Falkiner-Rose, to bring this book to fruition.

The Australian Business Deans Council (ABDC) Executive Committee

Caroline Falshaw, ABDC Executive Officer for many forms of logistical support and proofreading

Lora Starling for book design and illustrations

Pam Kershaw for editing

Zara Falkiner-Rose for book layout and her strong contribution to the social media section

Belinda Nemec for indexing

The following experts were very generous in sharing their time and insights

Professor Carl Rhodes, *University of Technology Sydney (UTS) Business School*

Catherine Webber, *Bond University*

Conor Duffy, *Australian Broadcasting Corporation*

Professor Debbie Haski-Leventhal, *Macquarie Business School*

Diane Shelton, *(former) CEO, Forethought Research*

Professor Elizabeth Sheedy, *Macquarie Business School*

Esme James, *Historian and PhD candidate, The University of Melbourne*

Professor Frederik Anseel, *The University of New South Wales (UNSW) Business School*

Dr Freya Higgins-Desbiolles, *University of South Australia (UniSA) Business School*

Professor Gary Mortimer, *Queensland University of Technology (QUT) Business School*

Dr Jason Pallant, *Swinburne Business School*

John Ross, *Times Higher Education*

Professor Julia Richardson, *Curtin Business School*

Julie Hare, *Australian Financial Review*

Kirsten Banks, *PhD candidate, The University of New South Wales (UNSW)*

Professor Kristy Muir, *(former) CEO, Centre for Social Impact, The University of New South Wales Business School (in conjunction with Swinburne University and The University of Western Australia)*

Dr Libby Sander, *Bond Business School*

Dr Louise Grimmer, *University of Tasmania (UTAS) Business School*

Professor Marian Baird AO, *The University of Sydney Business School*

Dr Michael Callaghan, *Deakin Business School*

Professor Nick Wailes, *The University of New South Wales (UNSW) Business School*

Associate Professor Nicole Hartley, *University of Queensland (UQ) Business School*

Peter Ryan OAM, *Australian Broadcasting Corporation*

Professor Peter van Onselen, *Griffith and University of Western Australia (UWA) Business Schools*

Professor Rae Cooper, *The University of Sydney Business School*

Professor Raymond Da Silva Rosa, *University of Western Australia (UWA) Business School*

Professor Richard Holden, *The University of New South Wales (UNSW) Business School*

Associate Professor Sarah Jane Kelly, *University of Queensland (UQ) Business School*

Stephen Matchett. *Campus Morning Mail*

Adjunct Professor Steve Worthington, *Swinburne Business School*

Professor Steven Rowley, *Curtin Business School*

Dr Stuart Middleton, *University of Queensland (UQ) Business School*

Tim Dodd, *The Australian*

Professor Tim Harcourt, *The University of Technology Sydney (UTS) Business School*

Adjunct Professor Warren Hogan, *University of Technology Sydney (UTS) Business School*

Why do we need this guide?

For some academics, translating their views and work to be easily understood by lay people can be akin to pulling teeth. For others, it's a rewarding and enjoyable experience, which can markedly boost their own public profile and that of their organisation.

There's no doubt that learning to operate in a world beyond academia may feel foreign and uncomfortable at first. But, as any traveller knows, building knowledge and having a mind open to adapting to new cultures does foster familiarity and confidence.

In this guide, academics from university business schools, who understand how to build strong public profiles and share their work widely, join journalists to discuss how to overcome communication challenges and create ongoing opportunities.

The Australian Business Deans Council has also delved into research and drawn on the ABDC communications advisor's 40-plus years of experience in journalism and strategic communication.

This guide drills down into working well with journalists and the best ways to communicate in mainstream and social media. Many topics are also of great relevance for building relationships with industry practitioners, funders, those working outside your academic discipline and others external to universities.

The ABDC hopes the wealth of insights, know-how and practical tips will help hone the skills of the more experienced and encourage tertiary students and early career researchers to dip their toes in the very public pool of knowledge so they can better convey their work, expert analysis and opinion.

1

Why communicate beyond your comfort zone?

Tin rattling, testing and telling it like it is

Picture this: you've had a good day. You have discovered something exciting and are dying to tell your nearest and dearest. At home you walk in to discover family members or friends intensely discussing an unrelated topic.

They look up, say 'hi' briefly, and go back to their conversation. There's no pause or easy opening in which to share your news. But you are passionate and determined so you quickly find a way to broadcast your message to the room.

There are several key ingredients here:

- You have something worthwhile to say
- That something matters to you and your audience
- You understand the key interests of those in your audience
- You know where they hang out and you meet them in that place
- You enthusiastically and knowledgeably explain why the news is important
- You concisely and clearly explain the key elements of the news
- You talk in language they all understand
- What you say resonates beyond the moment you say it.

If you can nail all those points in all your communications and know how to effectively distribute your messages, then you can probably stop reading now. After all, there are no secret ingredients or dark arts at work here.

However, while the principles are straightforward, there are endless variations on the themes. Communicating well is always a work in progress that changes with each circumstance, topic, platform and medium used.

CHAPTER 1

How to be relevant

- Why your research findings need a wider reach

- You have a head start with media because academics are trusted

- Yes, we're talking about how marketing can meet scholarship

- It's not dumbing down, it's using a different language

- Why you should contribute to public and policy conversations

Defining what makes a person and their work relevant is highly subjective but hugely important.

Traditionally, academics have sought relevance within international research communities and higher education institutions, building on the work of one another and staying abreast of deep research being conducted in their field.

Promotions have been heavily influenced by academics' articles and citations in the highly ranked peer-reviewed journals that are key to boosting individual reputations and university rankings.

However, for those outside universities, articles in peer-reviewed journals are often of limited or little use.

Without external promotion the dissemination of research findings may be confined to expert circles.

There is a global move towards more open access but, for those without academic journal subscriptions, the cost of one journal paper locked behind a paywall is often more than they are used to paying for an entire book.

Usually, journal papers are published a year or two after research is completed which – depending on the topic – can make the papers more of historical interest than contemporary relevance to practitioners.

And then there's the format of the journal articles themselves, with vital but lengthy explanations of the rigorous research methodology and a writing style that can be user-friendly only to experts already in the know.

Policymakers, influencers, industry practitioners, journalists and their audiences often need only the key points of the issue in language they understand and in a form that is easily and quickly digestible.

Some view this as 'dumbing down' academic work and providing simplistic explanations that scratch merely the surface of complex issues.

There are also many times when academics have dropped everything to talk to a deadline-riding journalist, only to find their thoughtful contribution reduced to a couple of paragraphs, several seconds on the airways, paraphrased without attribution or not used at all.

So why would anyone put their research and decades of expert knowledge out there only to become a zephyr sucked into the never-ending tornado of 24/7 news? Or to have their work cherry-picked to provide academic credibility to policies and external parties over whom the experts have no control?

Communicating publicly, through the media and other forums, can have unpredictable positive and negative results. However, no one will know and comprehend what you are doing unless you tell them in a way they understand. This, in itself, may be reason enough to reach outside your immediate sphere.

There's also the view that public funding brings with it an obligation for universities and academics to work for the public good, which requires external engagement and communication.

John Ross, Asia-Pacific Editor of *Times Higher Education*, says: 'Academics live in the real world and they want to solve real world problems, so it's important for them to engage.'

But academic research which stays contained in some sort of academic bubble of well-written and well-crafted journal publications isn't going to have much impact.

'Academics live in a very competitive field – ever more competitive – and they need as many quivers in their bow as possible to demonstrate their worth,' Ross says.

'What's the point of being an academic if nobody's actually going to read your work? The best way to get people to read your work is to get it out there, and the media are a major source of that,' says Steven Rowley of Curtin Business School.

The National Education Reporter of the Australian Broadcasting Corporation (ABC), Conor Duffy, agrees that the reach of mass media is vital to academics who want to showcase their best work and put the case for public investment in universities.

Business school subjects touch many parts of our lives

Most of the academics interviewed for this book represent many of the areas of expertise that come under the umbrella of business schools. Their subjects go to the heart of how we work, live and play – like economics, finance, tourism, sports management, leadership, human resources and the culture of organisations – all of which makes academics in business schools more suited to democratic debate than many other disciplines.

'You could follow what's going on in the media and you could connect it to virtually every area of management and commercial study – whether you're an accountant, a marketer, in digital marketing, social media, operations, supply chain or management. Whatever it is, you can absolutely connect it,' Julia Richardson of Curtin Business School says.

'It's not just about us and it's not just about us churning out academic publications. It's about giving back to the community that is giving to us.'

Mark Reed of Newcastle University in the UK says: 'Put simply, research impact is the good that researchers can do in the world. What is the good you can do?'[1]

Really? You're talking marketing?

Critical to demonstrating relevance is being able to highlight what you are doing to audiences outside academe, and it is here where marketing can meet scholarship.

" Whether we're talking about traditional businesses, small businesses, social enterprises, not-for-profits, those organisational structures are really important to how we function and how the economy functions, how we function socially, how we market to different ideas, how our behaviour is influenced, who it affects, who employs, what kind of leaders do we have, what kind of leadership do we need? How do we strategise around some of these things? What does this look like from a cultural sense and how are we sustainable so that we can do all these things that we love and need as a society while also making sure that we have a [healthy] environment, climate and are connected to Country? "

KRISTY MUIR, *(FORMER) CEO, CENTRE FOR SOCIAL IMPACT, UNSW BUSINESS SCHOOL*

Many scholars envisage marketing solely as sell-the-university material in websites, advertisements and Open Day brochures. But let's take the view that marketing is much more than commercial promotion.

Marketing expert, Seth Godin says: 'Marketing is the generous act of helping someone solve a problem. Their problem. It's a chance to change the culture for the better. Marketing involves very little in the way of shouting, hustling, or coercion. It's a chance to serve, instead.'[2]

Bernadette Jiwa, who specialises in storytelling in business innovation and marketing, maintains that 'ideas in isolation are worthless; if they have no impact, then they don't matter. Creation, innovation and entrepreneurship are not just about putting stuff out into the world — art and business alike are about doing things that make a difference.'

The start of all effective marketing is understanding what matters to you and your potential audiences so people will have a reason to stop and take in what you want to communicate.

John Ross of *Times Higher Education* says: 'Whether you want to build a profile or whether you want to publicise and increase the impact of this big piece of work you've just done, it's the same thing really. You need to identify what it is about the work that you've done that makes it of interest to a wide audience and then you need to find a way of communicating that.'

❝ One of the biggest challenges an entrepreneur or innovator has is understanding how to make [their] ideas resonate. We tend to have no shortage of ideas, but we struggle to tell the story of how they are going to be useful in the world and why they will matter to people. Marketing is the way we communicate how our ideas translate to value for people in a marketplace.[3] ❞

BERNADETTE JIWA, *AUTHOR OF MARKETING: A LOVE STORY*

Economist Warren Hogan of UTS Business School has been speaking to journalists for so long that he just sees it as part of his role.

'It's about giving the broader community an understanding that these business schools are business. They're highly academic. They are trying to get published. They're teaching, and they are really focused on that. But they're also engaging and trying to get the right kids to come and study,' Adjunct Professor Hogan says.

He believes that trust in academics has held up better than trust in those employed commercially in areas like banking. 'Therefore, academics have an opportunity and an obligation, I would argue, to utilise that trust.'

A 2021 Grattan Institute report[4] on removing barriers to policy reform says government is usually better when popular views are tempered by expert institutions, because populations tend to trust experts much more than politicians.

UTS Business School's Carl Rhodes says people value academic views because academics do not have to toe a company line.

'So, I might say one thing when you call me up, and then you might call one of my colleagues down the hall who will say something of a completely different political persuasion and different opinion. If you speak to me, I'm representing myself as Professor Carl Rhodes, who happens to work at UTS, and that's where the value is added.'

Freya Higgins-Desbiolles, of the UniSA Business School believes there's a role for all ways of looking at the world.

'I have some people that I disagree with strongly, but I still support their work because I believe that we're all contributing to the conversation and we shouldn't be speaking in echo chambers – which is why this public interface is so important.'

Nick Wailes, of the UNSW Australian Graduate School of Management, says: 'It's a critical role for the universities to be actively involved in the debates about our society and how we're shaping it and, if we have expertise and insight, we should be thinking about sharing that.

'Whether you want to call that engagement or impact, it's still core to our mission and it's also core to our ongoing relevance,' Professor Wailes says.

So are academics contributing enough to wider public and policy conversations?

The COVID pandemic highlighted the vital role of university researchers in finding solutions to life-threatening issues. However, the higher education crisis stemming from the impact of lock downs and closed international borders made it all the more important for universities to communicate their worth.

'We should use it as an opportunity to grow and change who we are and the way that we interact with external stakeholders. Many universities say that they do. Very few do it well,' Debbie Haski-Leventhal of Macquarie Business School says.

Journalists interviewed for this guide expressed concern about the decline in access to university leaders and the layers of spin between them asking questions and the often meaningless answers given in response.

One former federal ministerial advisor suggested that universities have, at times, been their own worst enemies by assuming their importance and focusing solely on what they want rather than the benefits they can provide.

He suggested it would be helpful if some leaders replaced hubris with a degree of humility and reflection on ways to improve university operations and their societal contributions. Failure to do so could undermine the efforts of individual academics and researchers in building external relationships.

Further fuelling the divide is the anti-expert populism, which has led to academics being chastised for not being real-world enough or being vilified for providing 'leftist' or 'elitist' opinions in debates such as those associated with Brexit, immigration and climate change.[4a]

Perhaps even worse is academic views being dismissed out of hand.

In 2014, *New York Times* columnist Nicholas Kristof caused a stir when he wrote: 'Some of the smartest thinkers on problems at home and around the world are university professors, but most of them just don't matter in today's great debates. The most stinging dismissal of a point is to say: *That's academic. In other words, to be a scholar is, often, to be irrelevant.*' [5]

Political editor Peter Van Onselen says there is currently an attack on political science and public policy expertise because politicians believe they know more than those who have studied political science and the processes around good public policy making. This is compounded by politicians 'barely listening to their public servants other than through a partisan lens', and the funding limitations imposed by politicians that see universities 'as cash cows at best.'

'The preferred antidote would actually be for the political class to respect scholarship and therefore fund adequately and allow academics to talk to each other in a way that continues higher learning. But like it or not, we've hit a point where it's become a little bit political for academics.'

" *If the academics don't engage then what they're doing will be typecast in an often-negative way by polemicists or politicians. I'm talking about commentators on media platforms who have axes to grind rather than an interesting and scholarly outcome.* "

PETER VAN ONSELEN, *UWA AND GRIFFITH BUSINESS SCHOOLS*

Do journalists have more intellectual traction than scholars?

'Much of the very best intellectual work being done in the United States is still being done by journalists, not scholars, and is still being published outside the university, by magazines and trade presses. Needless to say, the thriving of exceptionally talented journalists is cause for nothing but celebration. But lately, with nearly everything about publishing in flux, the relationship between intellectuals and the public is more vexed than ever.' [6]

Jill Lepore The New Economy of Letters

Thought leaders and public intellectuals

Political scientist Daniel Drezner makes the distinction between 'public intellectuals' and 'thought leaders' who have very different styles and purposes in a marketplace where ideas are the currency.

66 *Public intellectuals know enough about many things to be able to point out intellectual charlatans. Thought leaders know one big thing and believe that their important idea will change the world.* [7] 99

PROFESSOR DANIEL DREZNER, *THE IDEAS INDUSTRY*

Unlike many public intellectuals, thought leaders excel in projecting the supreme confidence that their ideas are correct. This confidence is cognitively satisfying to audiences; even critics of thought leaders acknowledge the seductiveness of their confident sales pitch, he says.

Professor Drezner posits that thought leaders are most rewarded because of three trends in the ideas marketplace: the polarisation of politics, the dramatic increase in economic inequality and the erosion of trust in authority. The diminished prestige of traditional titles, awards and accreditations means that, even in a marketplace receptive to new ideas and communication pathways, public intellectuals must work harder to make their voices heard.

The public intellectual serves a vital purpose in democratic discourse: exposing shibboleths masquerading as accepted wisdom. Public intellectuals are critics and critiquing those who hawk bad policy wares is a necessary function in a democracy.

'A public intellectual's greatest contribution to the marketplace of ideas is to point out when an emperor has no clothes. When public intellectuals lose their prestige, it becomes that much easier for politicians or charlatans to advance an idea into the public consciousness – regardless of its intrinsic merits – through sheer, unflagging will,' Professor Drezner says.[7]

" We are living in an age where people are so ready to believe things which are utterly wrong so it's really important that academics are bastions of the truth. By truth, I don't mean that everyone necessarily knows what's true, but they have to be utterly committed to the principle that conclusions are tested…and that we have to be ready to throw away even an idea that we hold dearly, if indeed it proves to be inconsistent with reality. "

TIM DODD, *HIGHER EDUCATION EDITOR, THE AUSTRALIAN*

1 Reed, MS. 2018, *The Research Impact Handbook*, 2nd Edition, Fast Track Impact, London.

2 Godin, S. 2018, *This is Marketing: You Can't Be Seen Until You Learn to See*, Penguin, New York.

3 Jiwa, B. 2014, *Marketing: A Love Story: How to Matter to Your Customer*, The Story of Telling Press, Melbourne.

4 Daley, J. 2021. *Gridlock. Removing barriers to policy reform*. Grattan Institute, Australia.

4a Fleming, P. 2021. *Dark Academia: How Universities Die*, Pluto Press, London.

5 Kristof, N. 2014. *Professors We Need You!* New York Times. Accessed at https://www.nytimes.com/2014/02/16/opinion/sunday/kristof-professors-we-need-you.html

6 Lepore, J. 2013. *The New Economy of Letters*. The Chronicle of Higher Education. Accessed at https://www.chronicle.com/article/The-New-Economy-of-Letters/141291.

7 Drezner, D. 2017. *The Ideas Industry: How Pessimists, Partisans and Plutocrats are Transforming the Marketplace of Ideas*. Oxford University Press, Oxford.

CHAPTER 2

Is the social licence of universities at stake?

- Your university knowledge should become a force for good

- Think broadly and don't just focus on peer-reviewed publications

- Stay relevant: engage in the new information realities

- Be explicit: how does your research relate to contemporary issues?

- Engaging with wider audiences may become a must-do, not a choice

There's a strong argument that public money is invested in tertiary education and reseach with the expectation that universities will create and share new and useful knowledge.

❝ *It really is about how we utilise who we are as an institution, our resources, our power, the amazing intellect that we have to make a difference. So academic institutions can become a force for good.* ❞

DEBBIE HASKI-LEVENTHAL, *MACQUARIE BUSINESS SCHOOL*

When reflecting on the role of the 'engaged scholar', Andrew R. Hoffman[8] argues that universities must learn to engage in new realities if they want to remain relevant in a world with many and varied new sources of information.

A decade ago, the then Vice-Chancellor of Australian Catholic University, Greg Craven, said Australian universities had been unable to 'articulate a vision of themselves to the public' and that they should be part of a 'constitutional social concept' that enables universities to 'stand as inhibitions to all power, be that media, government or business.'[9]

However, after 17 years working in higher education, journalist Julie Hare of the *Australian Financial Review* says university leaders have become less willing to engage publicly.

'I think there's a great fear of retribution by governments and by organisations if they don't say the right thing. So, this whole kind of freedom of speech thing is quite odd in that I think there's a lot of people who don't feel comfortable at all speaking,' she says.

'The number of vice chancellors, when I started writing about this, who were free and willing to engage in conversation and express their opinion has now diminished. Basically, they defer back to the lobby groups [like Universities Australia]. It's very hard to get a vice chancellor (VC) on the record with an opinion these days,' Hare says.

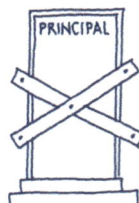

The ABC's Conor Duffy says he goes to one VC regularly because he's had so many knock backs from others, 'or when they have granted an interview it's kind of incomprehensible to everyday audiences.'

But while some university leaders may shy away from putting their heads above the political parapets, there are many other ways that academics can and do show the value of their work.

In the book *Whackademia*,[10] Richard Hill says: 'Occasionally academics do venture beyond university precincts and may sit on boards, inquiries and management committees, offer their advice to industry, present papers at conferences, act as advocates and give occasional media interviews. However, for many academics community service may not even figure as part of their workload calculations.'

Do they know what you do?

Bond Business School's Libby Sander says it's easy to assume that people will understand the results of her research and how it applies to the world.

This isn't true, so universities do have to be explicit in showing how research will actually relate to those industry issues or some more general issues in society. There are many business research topics that are very significant to issues that are happening in the world, she says.

University of Tasmania (UTAS) Business School's Louise Grimmer and all other academics interviewed for this guide are passionate about widely sharing their expertise.

Dr Grimmer's work involves public lectures, public talks, writing op-eds, writing pieces for *The Conversation*, doing radio interviews and other activities that that give back to the community that pays academic wages.

'Also, we're researching things that are important for the public and society. There's no point doing that stuck in an ivory tower and then distancing ourselves from everyone,' she says.

Professor Daniel Drezner[11] says many of the skills needed to thrive in the public sphere – speed, clarity, wit and the ability to provide self-assured, real-time analysis – are different from those of academic scholarship, which requires original research, careful fact-checking, rigorous peer review and citations to authoritative and relevant literature.

He argues that academics in their formative years are taught to focus exclusively on writing for fellow academics in peer-reviewed publications.

When they are asked later to communicate more widely, 'it is unrealistic to expect them to suddenly exercise communication muscles that have atrophied for decades. It would be like asking a world-class basketball player to excel at baseball because he loved the sport as a kid.'

He contends that the upside for an adjunct professor, graduate student or lay person may be that they realise they have much more power communicating outside academe because the modern ideas industry rewards intellectuals who are willing to engage a wider audience.

While some scholars might excel at both tasks, it is more likely that some professors will be better at public outreach than others. These skills create new pathways to public recognition beyond the control of traditional academic gatekeepers.

Promoting incentives

Many still think that wider engagement and impact are being stymied partly by academic promotion being inextricably linked to citations and publishing in highly ranked academic publications, rather than evidence of impact.

In the report, *Gridlock. Removing barriers to policy reform*[12], John Daley says academics would be more likely to champion reforms if universities changed their criteria for employment, performance management and promotion to focus more on involvement in policy processes – such as submissions to parliamentary committees – rather than refereed journal articles.

'It would also help if universities created incentives to focus more on domestic policy problems (typically discussed in local journals) rather than the more general problems typically discussed in prestigious international journals that typically count for more in academic hiring and promotion decisions. Universities may be more likely to make these changes if the Commonwealth Government changes the incentives it imposes on universities accordingly, Daley says.

Debbie Haski-Leventhal of Macquarie University agrees: 'The narrative of how we're making a difference, how we are serving the community, how we are becoming a force for good, is usually left out of the applications for promotion. We always talk about, and I see, people promoted just on the basis of their research citations. So even when we talk about research impact at universities, what we're actually looking at is research outputs, at how much we're publishing in journals. Not the way that our research is helping to shape the community, society, industry.'

As the author of *The Purpose-Driven University*,[13] she asks how are we changing people's minds? How will we contribute to improving humanity and addressing the social issues that we're currently facing?

Professor Haski-Leventhal says some universities are really changing their discourse but, as long as most universities are looking very narrowly at their role as conducting research and teaching students, they will not be able to come out of the boundaries that they set themselves.

Nevertheless, the days when you could sit in your office and produce technical papers for a very small community are coming to an end very quickly, UNSW Business School's Nick Wailes says.

In the past few years, he has had the opportunity to sit on university promotion committees where it is very clear that people's ability to communicate effectively with a broader stakeholder community is becoming a critical part of senior roles. 'What's been the impact of their research? Have they engaged with the broader stakeholder group? What changes or outcomes are a result of that?' Wailes says.

Sarah Jane Kelly of UQ Business School carries out appraisals of academics and asks: '*Tell me in a measurable way what you're doing a day a week towards service and citizenship*. It can be things like translating your research, working with industry more closely etc.'

8 Hoffman, A.J. 2016, Reflections: Academia's Emerging Crisis of Relevance and the Consequent Role of the Engaged Scholar, *Journal of Change Management*, vol. 16, no. 2, pp. 77-96

9 As cited on page 22 of Hill, R. 2012. *Whackademia: An Insider's Account of the Troubled University*, New South Books, Sydney.

10 Ibid

11 Drezner, D.W. 2017. *The Ideas Industry: How Pessimists, Partisans, and Plutocrats are Transforming the Marketplace of Ideas*, Oxford University Press, Oxford.

12 Daley, J. 2021. *Gridlock. Removing Barriers to Policy Reform*. Grattan Institute. Australia.

13 Haski-Leventhal, D. 2020. *The Purpose-Driven University: Transforming Lives and Creating Impact through Academic Social Responsibility*. Emerald Publishing. Australia.

CHAPTER 3

Communicating for you and your institution

- Why should you build your profile with industry and media?

- Are you a university for the real world and a magnet for students?

- Remember: not everyone reads higher education supplements

- If students Google you, do they see a strong media profile that adds legitimacy and currency to your academic work?

- Have you got the balance right: is your material well written and engaging?

Communicating well can benefit individual academics and their institutions.

Michael Callaghan of Deakin Business School says his marketing background makes him see the value of lifting the university's profile every time its name is in the media. It provides free publicity that can equate to tens of thousands of dollars in advertising.

'So even if it's just a puff piece that's being written on a Sunday afternoon about a particular consumer issue, I will comment about it because of an obligation to my employer to show the relevance of Deakin University in terms of actually commentating on issues that are important to the average consumer,' he says.

Professor Gary Mortimer hopes that his industry background and presence in the media with frequent mentions of QUT Business School, encourages students to go to QUT.

Professor Warren Hogan believes he is helping UTS Business School if a couple of parents, who hear him talking about current events, think: *'That wouldn't be a bad place for our kid to go after they finish high school. They've got academics who are getting published and that's a good, well-rounded place for the young person to be'.*

Swinburne Business School's Jason Pallant knows that the first thing that some students do is Google him. Being quoted in, or writing for, the media adds legitimacy and relevance to his teaching and can have a positive impact on research partnerships.

However, it can be a balancing act

Campus Morning Mail Editor, Stephen Matchett, says academics taken seriously in their area of expertise also have the challenge of broadening that field and reaching more people.

A lot of material from universities is well-written but not always very engaging, which he puts down to the 'academic fear of being criticised by their colleagues for not covering every possible eventuality, and not writing in the passive tense. And on the other hand, you've got the universities who are thinking: *Good Lord. That may be taken by the government to criticise their policy on nuclear power. A combination of this makes it hard.'*

*Communicating well can benefit
individual academics and their
institutions.*

CHAPTER 4

Speaking to industry

- Why you should aim for more partnerships and industry engagement

- How to get out of your comfort zone and create networks

- Look for collaborations that can drive greater industry funding

- The importance of advocacy and strategy of those who have credibility and experience in industry and academia

- What's the value of broader engagement and impact?

- Tip: the case study that drove one academic's most influential academic paper

> **"** When I came to QUT, the one thing that struck me is that there are academics doing amazing research, cutting edge research that industry is hungry for. But when I was in industry, I had no idea of the level of research, information and data that was available. **"**

PROFESSOR GARY MORTIMER, *QUT BUSINESS SCHOOL*

The drop in international student revenue caused by COVID-19 restrictions put pressure on universities to look for alternative avenues of engagement and funding. This in turn has pushed academics globally to engage with industry and social communities.

One of the barriers to this stems from the historic academic focus on individuals flourishing and competing with one another. 'You get promoted off the back of your work, not the work you do in partnership with others,' Professor Kristy Muir, formerly of the Centre for Social Impact at UNSW, says.

Professor Muir says institutions funded largely by the provision of education have not been forced to make business research accessible to the world.

'We haven't had to be as driven by partnerships and engagement with industry. But I think this is a cross section in time where we can start to do that differently – and it works,' she says.

Carl Rhodes of UTS Business School wants to see a change in the idea that the only thing of academic value is publishing articles in relatively arcane journals.

'What kind of values are we promoting as the leaders of business schools? If it comes down to brownie points or a specific kind of politics of incentives, then let's start giving some brownie points for a broader range of things. What we're trying to do here at UTS is to really show the value in this broader level of engagement.'

Julia Richardson of Curtin Business School says universities have a responsibility to work with industry to disseminate useful information. Doing that effectively requires higher degree research (HDR) training and support and training for junior academics to move away from a covert approach to a more open, collaborative approach.

Overcoming competitive barriers

One major handbrake on academics sharing information is concern, or even paranoia, about potential theft of their work.

'We were trained to always hold on to our intellectual property so, until you've got that journal article, don't share it with anyone. And if you've got it in a conference paper, don't give away all your data,' Nicole Hartley of UQ Business School says.

'Unfortunately, that comes from instances where people are plagiarising and stealing your ideas, then suddenly you've got someone who moves really quickly, they've done that study and they've got it published.'

Researchers have only one chance with academic publishing and once someone has published, that's it. 'So no matter how many years you've worked on it, particularly if you've got a big grant, you hold your cards close to your chest,' she says.

However, Associate Professor Hartley thinks changes are coming as younger academics are more inclined to 'give feedback and help you, then go off and do their own thing'. This compares to the former 'very dog-eat-dog kind of environment.'

Professor Carl Rhodes doesn't see anything wrong with sharing outcomes of research early. 'To work with a partner, and to suggest you're not going to share anything preliminary, would strike me as being a little bit precious on the part of the academic,' he says.

Jason Pallant of Swinburne Business School looks at tailoring the information he gives out to specific audiences, carving up different pieces to go in different ways.

In the past, Dr Pallant has provided top-line or preliminary trends or general findings to public or commercial audiences that just want to be pointed in the right direction. That work does not conflict with his academic journal articles that require much greater detail.

Academics interviewed have suggested more associations or networks could show the benefits of cooperation. They also note there is a level of obligation to share information because a lot of research is taxpayer funded.

Traversing publishing, teaching and industry engagement

Another barrier can be the innate ability of individuals, however the skills required for engagement and external communication can be learned.

Professor Warren Hogan doesn't think it's easy for academics to be good at everything. The teaching skill set is critical – that has many dimensions in itself – and it is a different skill set to publishing. External engagement and impact is another skill set which is the least explicit and valued.

He says institutions need to identify people's real strengths. 'A lot more work needs to be done to make the rubber hit the road, so to speak. Words are one thing, but you've got to do something really quite profound in terms of people's structures around their work.'

Some researchers may be intimidated by having to work with, rather than for, those interested in their field. 'It is hard enough working out who might be interested in our work, let alone having the confidence to actually connect with them,' Professor Mark Reed says.[14]

On a more positive note, he knows many researchers who grudgingly started engaging with people who were interested in their research, and who then discovered those relationships led to new collaborations and funding. Those projects led to new discoveries, which in turn fuelled the sense of curiosity that first brought them into research.

EXAMPLE

Debbie Haski-Leventhal says, after joining Macquarie University, she created a network of 34 leading Australian companies working together to enhance research on corporate social responsibility. It ran for four years.

'We had workshops. We had events in Parliament House. We had reports. We did research together. We were looking at what was interesting to them and that opened me up to having all this feedback of *"This is how your research impacted our work."* But to be able to do that, I had to get out of my comfort zone – which was very hard – and work with these companies and create ongoing engagement with external stakeholders.'

Is the question and the research relevant?

In terms of engagement, it can be important to choose research questions that are relevant to practitioners to avoid losing their interest.

However, while choosing relevant questions is one thing, conducting relevant research may be another[15] thing entirely.

To work closely with industry, Rae Cooper of The University of Sydney Business School's team is talking to young women about the design of surveys that underpin research on the women's views on their current and future work.

'So we are talking to young women about how to form the questions, but also doing interviews with industry colleagues about what is happening at the moment, what matters to them, what are the key areas of action that they seeing. We tend to do that very early and all the way through our research projects,' Professor Cooper says.

In a paper on *Enhancing the Practical Relevance of Research*[16], Michael Toffel contends that relevant research should highlight findings and use specific examples that encourage practitioners to act. This means including – and taking quite seriously – an *implications for practice* section in papers.

EXAMPLE

About five years ago, Professor Carl Rhodes of UTS Business School wrote an article for an important journal in his field of organisational studies. The journal sent him a 'revise and re-submit' response with no guarantee the article would be published. The journal liked the ideas around the role of corporations in democracy but said Professor Rhodes had not included an example.

At that time, he had been commenting on the Volkswagen diesel emissions scandal in the media. The scandal was exactly the case study he needed. He incorporated the media coverage into the article called 'Democratic Business Ethics', which has become his most influential academic paper.

Professor Rhodes says the case demonstrates how media and academic work are not necessarily separate.

'Speaking to people in public and to journalists about ideas that are based on your work means that you have to qualify those ideas. You need to explain them, you need to think them through, and it actually helps develop the intellectual work,' he says.

Tackling time-based tensions

Peter Van Onselen of UWA and Griffith Business Schools says there is a cultural attitude to overcome in organisations that see engagement with academic researchers as a time waster because it slows down getting to market or slows down the public policy making process.

No doubt there can be tensions between those in industry who want quick, actionable results, and academics whose training has emphasised not releasing research results until they have been peer reviewed.

Professor Steven Rowley says practitioners do not want a scenario of *'we'll give you 50 grand now…and then it's two, three years down the track'* before they get results. That's why partnerships, which help deliver research as quickly as possible, are important.

Professor Kristy Muir suggests a drip-feed approach, using the example from years of research on financial resilience done by the Centre for Social Impact with the National Australia Bank.

'So we might take a piece that says *this is why financial resilience matters to the world* and I can do an interview on ABC Radio that says: *financial resilience matters because if you don't have enough money when your fridge dies, your washing machine falls over and that lands you in front of the payday lenders. You can get in these loops of having to borrow cash, paying back too much money.'*

Professor Muir says that creates a narrative about why that piece of research matters before the research is finished or the data peer reviewed. The research team can then release findings at different stages of the work.

Talking their language

The practitioner academic or *pracademic* with experience and credibility in academia and industry can be a powerful advocate and strategist for improving industry and university engagement.

Gary Mortimer of QUT Business School worked for retailers and with industry associations before entering academia a decade ago. This gave him a firm foundation from which to develop and share research through invited industry presentations, industry reports and in media as an opinion leader. Almost all his academic research has been funded by industry.

'Coming out of industry is helpful because we tend to talk two different languages: industry versus academia. But certainly, I would attribute all of my research funding from engaging in industry and working on industry projects that are collaborative. That's not only impactful research that might change policy or procedures in some way for retail, but also generating new knowledge for academia,' Professor Mortimer says.

As a PhD student, Libby Sander of Bond University was told she was not communicating well unless she could explain her thesis to her grandmother in two minutes.

'We tell our PhD students that and it applies to ourselves as well. We have to be able to communicate clearly to industry because they don't talk like we do. They don't write like we do.'

One of her students is now a change management consultant and her firm presents reports in PowerPoint, demonstrating the attention span and the format top industries and businesses use. 'No one's going to read a 100-page report unless it's a Royal Commission or something major,' Dr Sander says.

Swinburne Business School's Jason Pallant prioritises communications to outlets he knows are read and valued by his industry targets.

If he shows how the department and faculty are doing relevant research, and communicates and disseminates it effectively, it helps build legitimacy of the research and can lead to research partnerships.

'In the past, I've had people from organisations reach out and say *I saw your piece on this, I found it really interesting, I would love to hear more about your research and opportunities.* That is a great win that can build partnerships and relationships moving forward,' Dr Pallant says.

EXAMPLE

INITIAL ENGAGEMENT THROUGH MEDIA

Freya Higgins-Desbiolles of UniSA Business School is involved with an events company that works with homeless women and helps get them back into the workforce while building their confidence and wellbeing. She was drawn to a woman she saw in the media, identifying her as a change maker. They created a partnership and have been working together since 2014. The academic work they do together informs her work and she uses it as evidence of her impact. 'I'm on call for her when she needs research to support the things that she's doing. She's a leader in the national and international space on women's leadership and social enterprises,' Dr Higgins-Desbiolles says.

Circling back to education

Sarah Jane Kelly of the UQ Business School emphasises that researchers also need to circle back to maintain a strong tie with teaching and learning.

'What are we in the business of doing? Well, we're in the business of educating people and leaders, whether they're in training for it or they're actually decision makers out there and leading in whatever sector organisation they're in,' Associate Professor Kelly says.

14 Reed, MS. 2018, *The Research Impact Handbook*, 2nd Edition, Fast Track Impact, London.
15 Toffel, MW. 2016, Enhancing the Practical Relevance of Research. *Production and Operations Management*, vol. 25, no. 9, pp. 1493-505.
16 Ibid

CHAPTER 5

Let's hear about your impact

- Will future funding follow outstanding academic impact?

- Research: what's the real-world application of your work?

- Think about your media narrative right at the start of your project

- Promote early outcomes so you can maintain engagement

- Capitalise on high impact to drive successful grant applications

Funding is being tied increasingly to performance measures that include significant levels of knowledge sharing.[17]

Global business school accreditation organisations, such as AACSB[18] and EQUIS, are also looking for impact beyond publication in academic journals, along with greater engagement with practitioners who will apply the research.

Steven Rowley of Curtin Business School thinks future research funding will probably follow those academics who are delivering wider impact. Young academics need to be very conscious of this because the days of writing a paper or two in a journal that perhaps not many readers are going to read will be gone fairly shortly. It is about making a difference, he says.

Professor Mark Reed[19] says generating new knowledge and making it available online is not enough; the data and information produced must be turned into knowledge with real world application. This requires patiently nurturing and developing two-way, trusting relationships. Academics need to really listen to, and learn from, those who may use their research.

This stands in stark contrast to the concept of *knowledge transfer*, which treats new knowledge as something that can be transmitted unchanged from one person to another. There are some situations where it is appropriate to simply communicate research findings but very few situations where some level of dialogue with stakeholders wouldn't improve the flow of knowledge, he says.

" By combining the efficient use of new media with everything we already know about working effectively with stakeholders and the public, we can do much, much more than ever before. "

PROFESSOR MARK REED, *THE RESEARCH IMPACT HANDBOOK*[9]

Funding for knowledge

The National Health and Medical Research Council's *Guide to Publication and Dissemination of Research* says[20] public funders expect institutions to encourage the widest possible dissemination of research, using effective modes, at the earliest opportunity.

Swinburne Business School's Jason Pallant has found his experience makes it relatively easy to explain on a grant application just how he will disseminate research results, because he has done it before.

'I say: *Like I have done with all of my other research recently. I will write a feature for this. I will do an episode on my podcast…*That becomes a lot easier if you've been doing those things because you prove you know how.'

In the early stages of valuable research, hypothesis development and linking the definition of a problem to literature of the relevant field are important, Deakin Business School's Michael Callaghan says.

'But in the back of our brains somebody in the research team really should be keeping an idea of what you're doing in terms of thinking: *What things are we doing here that are going to have practical implications and actually are going to be interesting enough to be reported in the media down the track?*'

The sooner you start thinking about the ways in which you can tell that narrative is very important, particularly when it comes to sourcing funding and generating some public relations and media about the research.

'It's understandable that governments and funding agencies really want to emphasise that there needs to be a relevant implication to whatever research that's being funded and undertaken,' he says.

In *The Research Impact Handbook*, Mark Reed outlines principles of impact. Paraphrased they are:

Design the impacts you want into research from the outset.

Represent systematically the needs and priorities of those who might be interested in or use your research.

Engage with empathy to build long-term, two-way, and trusting relationships so you can ideally co-generate new knowledge.

Show early impact. Many people researchers work with expect impacts in weeks and months. Partly this is about managing expectations, but it is also about trying your best to deliver tangible results as soon as possible, which can help keep people engaged with your work.

Reflect and sustain. Keep track of what works, so you can improve your knowledge exchange, continue nurturing relationships and generate impacts. Avoid repeating the mistakes of others when you share what works – as well as your failures – with colleagues.

Keep asking who benefits and how.

❝ *People regularly ask me when does the 'pathway to impact' stop and the impact begin? The answer is that impact starts when you see benefits.* ❞

PROFESSOR MARK REED, *THE RESEARCH IMPACT HANDBOOK*

17 Tsui, L, Chapman, SA, Schnirer. L & Stewart, S. 2006, *A Handbook on Knowledge Sharing: Strategies and Recommendations for Researchers, Policymakers, and Service Providers*, Community-University Partnership for the Study of Children, Youth, and Families, Alberta. Canada.
18 AACSB. 2012. *Impact of Research A Guide for Business Schools Insights from the AACSB International Impact of Research Exploratory Study*. Accessed at http://www.aacsb.edu/-/media/aacsb/publications/research-reports/impact-of-research-exploratory-study.ashx?la=en
19 Reed, MS. 2018, *The Research Impact Handbook*, 2nd Edition, Fast Track Impact, London.
20 National Health and Medical Research Council. 2020. *Publication and Dissemination of Research a Guide Supporting the Australian Code for the Responsible Conduct of Research*. Australia.

Abx(123)
2x(ab)Z $\rightarrow$

Engage with empathy to build long-term, two-way, and trusting relationships so you can ideally co-generate new knowledge.

CHAPTER 6

Reaching policymakers

- Remember that policymakers need independent, high-quality research

- How and why academics should play a huge role in advising policymakers

- Experts say there are five pathways to reach policymakers

- Should you be political but not partisan?

- Strategies you can use to impact public debate and policy

Karen Mills, former administrator of the US Small Business Administration and now a senior fellow at Harvard Business School, has emphasised that providing time-poor, fast-moving policymakers with access to independent, high-quality research from outside sources can make a real difference both in developing good policies and in getting broad-based support for their implementation.[21]

'The truth is that the comparative advantage of scholars, in general, is in producing research, not just opinions. They can have tremendous impact when bringing that research to bear on vital problems facing the nation and the world,[22]' Professor Mills says.

Professor Peter Van Onselen, of UWA and Griffith Business Schools, says politicians have a view that, if a department comes up with an idea of how to do business, they'll take it or reject it based on political decision making.

'They will look to have it tested in a case-study way, but they won't have it tested in a scholarly way. It's entirely different to [it] being done by proper research academics who have expertise in the area, sometimes through a public policy making process. They'll seek that consultation, but often it's an afterthought or a box-ticking exercise.'

Tim Dodd, Higher Education Editor at *The Australian*, says the hollowing out of the expertise in, and politicisation of, the public service is an issue along with the rising power of political advisors who may be inexperienced in policy making. He sees a huge role – ideally played by academics with expertise in their field – in advising people who are devising policies. But that does not happen enough.

'It's something that everyone has to work at – from those in government, to those in academia, to those in the media, to those who have any sort of a platform or influence. We all have to open ourselves up to looking for answers that work and which are based on evidence rather than just going with what's popular, what's trending, what is coming out of the focus groups or whatever,' he says.

Associate Professor Steven Rowley believes the difficulty of communicating directly with policymakers means relying on your research publications reaching them, which can sometimes happen through the links of research funders or platforms like LinkedIn.

As policymakers generally just want a number and *'this policy will impact on X by Y'*, the executive summaries of research or media releases can be useful for them.

'We learnt pretty early on that the policy makers just want a couple of nice juicy headlines that they can use to support their work. And quite often they won't even recognise your work or acknowledge you, but you can see it in the documents,' Associate Professor Rowley says.

This can be frustrating for researchers trying to demonstrate the impact of their work.

Being political but not partisan

The University of Sydney Business School's Rae Cooper emphasises the need to rely on your research, your data, your own insights and your research team. But it can be valuable to cite the work of others around the topic at hand.

'It's important to speak genuinely and authentically to what we know about and then politicians can do their political work if they want to. We're not there to advocate for any group, but we might. That's not to stop us from having a particular view about the way that the world may be a better place in particular ways informed by our research.'

Generally, she won't back down, even if it's around controversial issues such as improving women's working lives, looking at issues around sexual harassment or women's labour force participation. Her research gives Professor Cooper confidence to hold her position.

Professor Kristy Muir, formerly of the Centre for Social Impact at UNSW, will always be political, as opposed to partisan, because her work involves understanding complex social problems and how we address them.

'How do we know what works, what doesn't, under what circumstances, and therefore how do we take that and affect change? And that means effecting change with and through not-for-profits, through governments at all levels, through corporate and social businesses, and social enterprises and philanthropy. So, in doing that, I have to be political because I have to understand what's material for whom, where the drive is, what's going to help get something over the line,' she says.

Professor Muir uses the example of sitting on the New South Wales Premier's Council on Homelessness. She understands the Premier's priorities and can attach the right evidence to support arguments to help address housing affordability and homelessness issues.

Pathways to policymakers

An analysis of 5% of the searchable database of impact case studies, compiled by the Higher Education Funding Council for England in 2015, found the impact pathways to policymakers most commonly cited by researchers, were:

- Publications – particularly peer-reviewed journals
- Advisory roles – contributing to government inquiries, reports, panels and committees
- Media coverage
- Partnerships and collaborations with industry and NGOs
- Presentations with industry, the public and government[23].

We can debate the merits of each pathway but, for many academics, media coverage is often the best bet in the absence of direct access to policymakers.

Media as the conduit

66 *The media has the power to change policy directions and decisions and get things done.* 99

JULIE HARE, *HIGHER EDUCATION EDITOR, AUSTRALIAN FINANCIAL REVIEW*

66 *We're far from setting policy on our own, but I think it certainly has an impact.* 99

CONOR DUFFY, *EDUCATION EDITOR, AUSTRALIAN BROADCASTING CORPORATION*

Most journalists interviewed for this guide are senior, higher education specialists. But in the report *Gridlock. Removing Barriers to Policy Reform*[24], John Daley says the role of popular opinion, markers of party loyalty, and vested interests in blocking policy reform is concentrated, sometimes hyper-partisan, and is morphing due to social media.

Daley says media coverage of policy issues tends to become less informed as declining advertising revenues cause cutbacks in newsrooms. Relatively uninformed journalists may gravitate towards the intuitive views of their audience (particularly if they are reinforced by vested interests), rather than writing articles to explain why reforms are worthwhile.

This trend may also contribute to the power of vested interests. With fewer specialised journalists, it is easier for well-resourced vested interests to drown out the public interest. A journalist who has not accumulated expertise in a policy area, and who is under pressure to publish and tweet about several stories per day, may be more inclined to reproduce uncritically the media release of a vested interest, rather than attempting to provide insight on the issues for their audience, Daley says.

This makes it all the more important for academics to share their expertise.

Economist Richard Holden of UNSW Business School, spent nearly a decade in the United States doing his PhD and then as a faculty member in American institutions. One of his motivations for returning to Australia was to have an impact on public debate and public policy.

'I actively sought out the ability to do some of these things. So it's been, to some degree, a conscious choice. And then that kind of creates its own opportunities and its own momentum and things go from there,' Professor Holden says.

Sometimes a politician or regulator will ask to discuss a piece Professor Holden has written for a newspaper.

'If you are in the fortunate position of being able to directly communicate with senior politicians, that's great', he says.

While almost nobody is going to be able to call up the Prime Minister or the Treasurer to discuss a particular issue, an article in a major newspaper may well be read.

'They might say, *that's stupid* or *I don't care* or *I already know that* or *I'm not going to do that.* But every now and then they say, Huh, I hadn't thought of that and get in contact,' he says.

LOCAL GOVERNMENT ENGAGEMENT

Dr Louise Grimmer of UTAS Business School says:
'I do work a lot with local councils, but that's because my name is out there in the media and that's how a lot of industry or government people find you. I did a report last year for Launceston City Council and all of the recommendations that I put in that report were adopted at a council meeting. So that's the impact. But it wouldn't have happened without the engagement that came first.'

Curtin Business School's Julia Richardson says policy makers are digesting media content, so it is important to give a very clear idea of what this means.

For example, more people are working from home. But practically speaking, what does that mean to the use of roads, city centres, real estate and so on? It must be sufficiently practical if the policy maker is going to want to talk to you.

Nicole Hartley of the UQ Business School says if you've been in *The Conversation* or you've been able to write a *Conversation*-style piece, you are stepping towards impacting public policy. That's because you can synthesise and strip down to the key relevance and impact behind your research, rather than justifying all the rigour behind it.

'Strip it down for *The Conversation* article, bring it back up for the policy,' she advises.

SOCIAL PROGRESS INDEX

Kristy Muir, formerly of the Centre for Social Impact at UNSW Business School, describes development of an Australian Social Progress Index that tracks social and environmental indicators using international methodological principles.

Professor Muir says: 'We communicated and worked with a whole bunch of employees in Federal Parliament to say: *We now have the Social Progress Index for Australia and we've got a history where we can predict your outcomes based on the postcode in which you live. And what would it mean to start to change that? What would it mean to start to improve that?*

Her team engaged federal employees across all government parties and had an impact with state and territory government levels working with different sides of politics.

'It's about the evidence and saying, *Here's the research. Here's the narrative that wraps around this research. Here's what happens if we might apply this and if we start to track that over time. Then let's see what kind of progress we can make against the commitments you're making as governments to these particular changes,*' Professor Muir says.

EXAMPLE

ACADEMIC ACTIVISM

Freya Higgins-Desbiolles entered academia from the development sector, with an activist mindset that has worked for her in the UniSA Business School. There is academic rigour to her activism, which focuses on host communities, tourism, human rights and social justice issues.

'One thing I did early, before I think the business schools were fully into it, was work on collaborative research projects in Aboriginal tourism.'

'So, I work with Aboriginal tourism operators in talking about what their interests are in tourism. One of the things that I've seen from their point of view is about the domestic market being racist. At the time that we were talking about it, it was very unpalatable to talk about that. And in my research with an Aboriginal operator, I did a research project with George Trevorrow of the Coorong Wilderness Lodge. It has been a key work in looking at Aboriginal tourism in Australia,' she says.

21 Blanding, M. 2015, *Business Research that Makes for Smarter Public Policy*. Harvard Business School.
22 Ibid
23 Ibid
24 Daley, J. 2021. *Gridlock. Removing Barriers to Policy Reform*. Grattan Institute. Melbourne. Australia.

WHAT SORT OF ACADEMIC RESEARCHER ARE YOU?

Determining your natural inclination to relate to external issues and stakeholders is part of the self-awareness needed to be an effective communicator. Inevitably some research topics and disciplines relate more readily to a wider public than others, but so does the way you conduct research and distribute its findings.

The following list, adapted from Roger Pielke Jr's five types of scientists[25] is one way to help situate yourself. Professor Pielke's archetypes are:

Honest Broker who provides as much information as possible on a particular topic and allows policymakers and the public to reduce the scope and make a decision.

Pure Scientist who focuses on research with no consideration for its use or utility (a role which he states is more frequently found in myth than practice).

Issue Advocate who focuses on the 'implications of research for a particular political agenda' and 'tends to reduce the scope of available choice'.

Science Arbiter who will answer questions from decision-makers to clarify research.[26]

Stealth Issue Advocate who seeks to hide his/her advocacy behind a facade of science. This 'is the fastest route to pathologically politicising science'... and 'gives scientists as advocates a bad name.'

25 Roger Pielke Jr. 2015. *Five Modes of Science Engagement*. Accessed at http://rogerpielkejr.blogspot.com/2015/01/five-modes-of-science-engagement.html
26 Hoffman, AJ. 2016, *Reflections: Academia's Emerging Crisis of Relevance and the Consequent Role of the Engaged Scholar*, Journal of Change Management, vol. 16, no. 2, pp. 77-96.

2

Understanding the media

CHAPTER 7

How media operate

- Why you should get to know the many-headed media beast

- Do you understand the media outlets that are relevant to your research?

- Contemporary newsroom operations: here's why deadlines are so tight

- Why you may need to be ready with an immediate response

- You can become a valued media source – here's how

It's not THE media. It's THOSE media

It's easy to fall into the trap of seeing the
media as one big beast when, in reality,
the media are made up of many outlets
with widely varied interests, audiences and
journalistic practices.

"*Journalists are no longer (if indeed they ever
were) a particularly definable tribe in terms
of the competencies, but also in terms of their
perceived function.* **"**

STEPHEN MATCHETT, *EDITOR, CAMPUS MORNING MAIL*

To get a feel for working with the media, it's worth
educating yourself. There are usually communications experts
in your university who should be able to assist, but your own
observations will provide a deeper understanding.

This does not require a major research project: you can
just consciously take note and make comparisons by reading,
listening and watching different media outlets – instead of
sticking to your favourites each day. Within those media outlets,
note which journalists are specialists or show a particular
interest in stories that encompass your areas of expertise.

The joy of the internet is that it's also never been easier
to access work by news and current affairs journalists and
presenters. This includes listening to parts of radio programs,
podcasts, television shows and appearances
on social media so you can work out the style
of interviewers you may encounter during
your work.

❝It's understanding the media and how it works… and also locating things in the real world…So what that means for a real person is X, Y and Z. How your research actually translates into everyday practice and how you can make a difference in people.❞

NICK WAILES, *UNSW BUSINESS SCHOOL*

A few basics on newsroom operations

Newsrooms and current affairs programs are usually dynamic environments occupied by those not afraid of saying what they think, often in very blunt terms.

At their heart are (metaphorically) the mother ships – usually called chiefs-of-staff, news editors or producers. They stay across everything that's happening and are the ones who assign specific people to cover stories. Those journalists, photographers and/or camera operators then act as little satellites; they go out and work reasonably autonomously, albeit reporting back in and receiving information from the mother ship in the office.

As stories go up and down in perceived importance during the day, those satellites can be sent off into different orbits. For example, one minute a journalist and camera operator may be covering a court case only to be diverted suddenly to a fire deemed more newsworthy.

News is always a work in progress so try not to take it personally if your interview or story is dropped at the last minute. There are many things happening in the world, and you can be easily pipped at the post by an unexpected event. If it's any consolation, there's every chance that the journalist who put the effort into the story is likely to be as miffed as you. If your story is not time sensitive, it may be held over to be used another day.

Stories can also be cut back or dropped because a live cross goes longer than expected on a news bulletin or some other breaking news interrupts the planned program. There may be fewer advertisers and therefore less money to support editorial pages in print publications – a lack of space that can, strangely, carry over to putting stories online.

'There's a prevailing attitude in print media that stories online have to look the same as stories in print. I don't understand this,' John Ross of *Times Higher Education* says. 'You want your stories to be as brief as is necessary to convey the important content, but I still don't quite understand why online stories can't be longer.'

John Ross says a story would rarely be dropped because of prejudice or a reaction to something said by an academic.

Testing times

To academics, tuned to semesters and research timelines, journalists can seem pushy, impatient and sometimes downright rude.

For their part, journalists can be frustrated by academics' lack of urgency when they are on tight deadlines and feeding multiple platforms.

'The really good academics that I interact with, a lot understand all of those pressures. They really do bend over backwards to help us out and that's really appreciated.' Conor Duffy, ABC Education Reporter says.

Catherine Webber, a former newspaper editor who is now Strategic Communications Advisor at Bond University, says you rarely find a journalist who doesn't want the expert and all the information they can get for whatever story they are working on. However, time is everything.

She says the lengthy academic peer-review process is the opposite of how journalists operate. The media need something 'incredible like five minutes ago'. If you go into a newspaper on a Friday morning, there could be 140 pages of emptiness and, within 12 hours, you filled that. That requires a lot of work and a lot of hunting down and trying to get the best experts and academics you can find, she says.

Steve Worthington of Swinburne Business School puts himself in the shoes of a journalist, whose job is to fill the blank spaces. He says the journalist may have media releases and other bits of information but can often benefit from an academic providing a quote from a 'totally neutral independent source' – and that provides an opportunity to connect.

'That story will be out in a couple of hours and if your quote is not in that story, the following day, there'll be a new story in its place,' Tim Dodd of *The Australian* says. 'So, if you're working in that sort of news cycle, then you need to give your information almost instantaneously. You might be able to think about it for five or 10 minutes before you have to talk but, after that, you'll have to talk.'

Academics and journalists both work very hard with long hours, John Ross of *Times Higher Education* says, but journalists are also doing 'much shorter pieces of work – 350, 550 words versus 6,000 words – that has to be done by 6pm rather than Thursday fortnight or something like that.'

Dealing with deadlines

Early on journalists are taught that it doesn't matter how good a story is, if it misses the deadline, it's worthless. Unlike the good old days, when there might have been three daily newspaper deadlines or one TV news deadline, today's deadlines are continuous because of the voracious online 24/7 news environment.

Conor Duffy says journalists do not want to ring someone up and demand that they drop everything and talk straight away. 'We always like to have more time with our stories. But in this media environment, where things are very sped up and newsrooms have reduced staff, there is often an enormous crunch at our end'.

'I will have multiple deadlines across television, radio and online now, whereas in the past, I might be able to prioritise one of those or at least just do two of those. For different newspapers that have their print edition, updating digitally through the day is probably how things have changed for them.

'In terms of logistics too, if I'm having to organise a television crew to come and interview someone, that's another whole layer of logistics and complications for me in terms of getting a crew to that person, sometimes in a different city to where I am, getting the material back to base, fed up a satellite to Sydney and then processed for TV, radio, and digital. So it's pretty lean,' Duffy says.

Deadlines are different for weekly or fortnightly programs or publications, and magazines can work months in advance. Therefore, it's always worth asking journalists about their time constraints.

Shrinking media doing more with less

In the past, journalism in traditional media was funded largely by advertising revenue. However, over the past decade, most advertising dollars have moved to online platforms like Facebook and Google. The result has been retrenchment of thousands of journalists and decimation of newsrooms around the world.

Many newsrooms are now trying to work with hugely reduced resources. Newspapers have been cut back radically in size. Other media outlets have closed and left behind *news deserts* particularly in regional areas.[28]

MOVING TARGETS

Journalist Peter Ryan is the Senior Business Correspondent for the ABC radio shows of *AM* and *The World Today,* as well as appearing on *Radio National Breakfast*.

Peter Ryan usually likes to get stories the day before, although sometimes stories will come to him days ahead, often with an embargo for the story not to be released until a particular date and time.

He says:'I got the first interview with the new ASIC boss.[27] That took me about three months to line up and I had a week's notice before I actually had to do the interview. But then you keep thinking *I know for sure something massive is going to happen that's going to knock this interview out of the way*. And actually, something really huge did happen and I couldn't get it on to AM. So I went to RN Breakfast and they said, *Sure, we'd like it*.'

Tim Dodd of *The Australian* describes some of the many changes he has seen since starting his journalism career in 1985.

'For the first 10 years of my career, there was no such thing as the internet. For the next 10 years, the internet was a thing where the stories in the paper were put as they were publishing the paper. It wasn't curated in any special way; it was just a dump of what was in the paper.

'Now everything's changed…more and more people read only on the internet so the internet has to come first.

'We have to keep on supplying stories during the day because people are going back

on to the website and the app all day and want to see fresh material. And they're interested in seeing a variety of materials. It's not just written stories. It's the videos, it's stuff that once us print journalists would never have conceived of doing.

'And all of this has happened at the same time as newsrooms have been cut drastically. It actually means that journalists have less time to investigate stories. They've generally got more time pressure on them now and they are having to do more work on different platforms at the same time. So that means that everything is done in more of a rush,' Dodd says.

Doing the rounds

There are two key types of reporters covering news and current affairs: specialists, who are on reporting rounds or beats, and general reporters who often have to be Jacks (or Jills) of all trades.

The specialists may have spent years building knowledge while covering areas such as police rounds, politics, education, business and sport, whereas it is not unusual for a general reporter to bone up on a story's background on the way to the job.

As a rule of thumb, specialists tend to be more senior reporters who cover mostly hard news, although having a title does not always mean they have vast experience in their designated area. They may have started on a particular round only the day before or, in larger rounds like federal politics, be the most junior member of a team.

The term 'editor' can also be a little misleading. The editor of an entire newspaper or a section like sport has a very different level of power than an editor who is, in reality, the main person on a reporting round. So just pay attention to who is doing what when you consume media.

“ For every journalist, it's very much a job where you learn on the job and you have to grow into things. ”

CONOR DUFFY, *ABC EDUCATION REPORTER*

Round advocacy

The upside of reporting rounds is the depth of expertise in the journalists and their ability to advise their bosses about the most important stories in their patch.

The ABC's Conor Duffy says many people don't realise that experienced rounds reporters are also often really good advocates on their behalf in newsrooms in terms of saying: *Actually it might seem like this, but there are very good and complex reasons why that isn't the case.* Although this may not happen so often with a rounds reporter 'who's very new and just kind of eager to please and doesn't feel confident and comfortable to challenge a request' from someone more senior.

Round journalists, who know what they are talking about, can ask more insightful questions. So 'when the minister says X, they can then say, *but wait a minute. You tried that in 1873 and that led to the Russian invasion of Crimea and so forth,' Campus Morning Mail* Editor, Stephen Matchett, says

However, being responsible for a round brings its own set of pressures. Round reporters are judged against the output of other specialist journalists in their area – and no one likes being scooped.

'Specialist reporters are under constant evaluation and having to meet various metrics to keep maintaining our existence,' Conor Duffy says. 'So it would be kind of a sad outcome if there weren't any education reporters left in Australia, but it's not a possibility that is completely remote or unlikely.'

Round capture

One downside of rounds is that familiarity with key players in an area can lead to what journalist Stephen Matchett describes as *round capture*.

'Reporting in any round, there is a risk of round capture: that journalists will become too close to people in the industry – not personally – but too close to the interests of an industry and people in it. That is one problem.

'Another problem is that they become so obsessed with the round that it becomes largely about the personalities rather than the policies…You make personal selections…inevitably your own interests creep in. I try not to do it in *Campus Morning Mail*, but they do,' he says.

'So there's always this tension of specialist journalists with the danger of one becoming too attached to the people on whom they're reporting.' However, Stephen Matchett says, really competent journalists are not captured by rounds. There are 'absolute stars who have been doing it for a long time and keep a distinct perception, a difference.'

27 Australian Securities and Investment Commission (ASIC)
28 See latest research at the Public Interest Journalism Initiative at piji.com.au

CHAPTER 8

What makes a news story?

- How to make your research appear fresh and interesting

- Hard and soft news – what's the difference and why does it matter?

- A 10-point assessment of your story's message and content

- What's the media value of your story: check it against these seven points

- How timeliness created a steaming hot story and really hit a nerve

In essence, a news story is something perceived to be new. That does not mean it is *actually new*; it just needs to be seen as new by the media outlet running it.

One of the great talents of those who package stories to pitch to the media is the ability to make something appear fresh and interesting. For example, each year for more than three decades, there has been a different take on red noses to boost free sources of publicity (aka media stories) for the annual Red Nose Day.[29]

A nose for news

Journalists develop the very subjective *news sense*. This can be most easily seen when all the journalists who attend the same media conference later highlight the same quotes that they, as individuals, deem to be the most newsworthy.

But while that sort of reportage can look like the media operating as a pack, journalists also spend a good deal of time trying to do outdo their journalistic competitors by digging for new stories or finding new angles on running issues.

To counter those who deliberately or inadvertently *bury the lead*, journalists also have a well-developed ability to read a paper or lengthy report very carefully before, as editor Stephen Matchett says, finding that footnote on page 137 is the story.

Is it a good little yarn?

Matchett quotes a colleague describing a news story as *a good little yarn*.

He asks: 'In this story, are there things that people don't know and they'll be interested to know? Is it written in a way that they will get what it's talking about quite quickly, and want to read to the end? That's hard to do. This is an entirely different function to those of scholarship.'

Hard and soft stories

There are roughly two types of media stories: hard and softer ones.

Hard stories must be covered. They include things like the release of the Consumer Price Index or unemployment figures, major findings of a Royal Commission, important political moves, Australians winning numerous gold medals in swimming at the Olympics, a major disaster and so forth.

Softer stories can range from research that is interesting, but not so ground-breaking that it must be reported immediately, to heart-warming human-interest stories, adorable animals or puff pieces about celebrities.

Weighing the value of a story

These elements of stories, adapted from a list by Denis Muller at the University of Melbourne, are useful ways to judge the weight likely to be given to a story.

The more of these, the bigger the media story:

MAGNITUDE (scale, impact)

NEGATIVITY (conflict, shock value, controversy)

PROXIMITY (geographic, social and/or cultural closeness to the audience)

TIMELINESS (recent event or new availability of information)

PROMINENCE (status, power of the information source or those involved in the story)

PERSONIFICATION (involvement of well-known people)

UNEXPECTEDNESS (man bites dog as opposed to dog bites man).

Tragedies, like the 2004 tsunami or the COVID-19 pandemic, cover all categories so it is no surprise when they dominate global news.

Assessing your story and messages

While university communications teams can be invaluable in gauging the newsworthiness of a suggested story, here are a few questions to ask yourself.

What is your story? What key points do you want to convey? If you can't explain it simply, do not expect anyone else to get it. With practice it is possible to convey three messages in 15 seconds – the length of many radio or television news grabs or quotes taken from interviews.

Will others find it interesting? This is where you need to take off the blinkers and be game enough to road test your potential story with people you would like to reach. If their eyes glaze over or they mouth half-hearted platitudes, you will probably need to adjust your approach or scrap the initial approach and come up with a better idea.

How far will your story travel? Has it got legs? This will help you approach the media outlets which best serve your potential audience.

- Is it of interest to your family only?
- Would it intrigue your neighbour or your whole street?

- Will those in your field of expertise, in academia or in industry, care?

- How about someone in your local community (be that social, geographical or cultural)?

- Would someone on the other side of your town or city give your story the time of day?

- What about someone living across your state?

- Would someone interstate find it worth a read, watch or listen?

- Is it a strong enough story to resonate with people overseas?

What makes your story different? Is it something of interest that we haven't heard before? Could you highlight the more novel part of your research to hook in the audience and lead them further into your story?

Have you looked for the human angle? Is there a good case history that will help to humanise and better explain an issue? We remember stories and people much more easily than we retain facts.

Can you make your story more topical by relating it to a newsworthy event? There's a day of the year for just about everything but only some of those days – like International Women's Day – are likely to help boost your related story. However, at the very least consider seasons, major events and prominent holidays. Even the universal birthday of horses on August 1 would be a good tie-in for an equine story.

Could you give your research a snappier title? There are an extraordinary number of research papers with deathly boring, convoluted titles that even a mother wouldn't love. There is a reason why headlines are important in the media:

they grab people's attention. You title doesn't have to be tabloid in taste, but it really helps if it's short, pithy, clever or, at the very least, to the point. (And, as an extension of that thinking, is the Abstract of your academic paper too abstract? Could it more pointedly convey what your paper is about?)

Have you chosen the right front person to promote your story? It may be diplomatic to stroke the ego of your boss but please include the person or people who can talk about the nitty gritty of the work and often provide the best quotes to journalists.

If your story is time-sensitive, are you releasing it at the best time? Are you likely to find your story overtaken by other, clearly predictable events? If that is the case, would it be sensible to rethink the timing?

Is there a story in your area that you have overlooked? People who work intensely in one area often take things for granted and overlook stories and information that those outside their sphere may find fascinating. Put yourself in outsiders' shoes and look at what you do with fresh eyes.

You may think this is obvious but...

It's extraordinary how often people forget these basic tenets:

Print needs good information

Radio needs sound and information

Television is looking for information, sound and bright, interesting, moving pictures

Online – the point of convergence – uses all.

Therefore, you can help to bolster a story by offering journalists, photographers and camera operators access to interesting images and audio that may be recorded in areas like production processes, meetings, events, and through data visualisations.

Media following media

The media follow the media – a situation that can see a rapid uptake of a story across the news landscape but, at worst, lead to rapid propagation of any mistakes in the original story.
In the past, print media would set the agenda for the day, radio would pick it up and then TV would come off the back of that. Indeed, one TV newsroom in Melbourne used to refer to a morning newspaper as the morning 'briefing notes'.

'If you've got a story in one media outlet other journalists will notice your work and, if the story is interesting enough, they'll probably pick it up,' the ABC's Conor Duffy says. Although there can be professional jealousies with journalists not wanting to be seen following each other.

Nevertheless, while print is still very influential, Conor Duffy thinks audiences now expect media outlets 'to bring more to the story and develop it in their own way'.

STEAMING HOT STORY

Nick Wailes of UNSW Business School wrote an op-ed about the closing of Starbucks in Australia that was published in the *Sydney Morning Herald* and also syndicated to other media.

Professor Wailes says: 'I did radio interviews with American National Public Radio, with the BBC, with the ABC. At one stage I had 85 media requests for comment. So that was quite demanding.

'I got to a certain point where I made a decision that I'd pull back because I thought *I've said what I wanted to say and my full-time job is not filling up newspapers or radio broadcasts,*' he says.

Creative Commons Licence to increase sharing

If you are looking for reach, Carl Rhodes of UTS Business School suggests seeking publication in an outlet such as *The Conversation*, which publishes with a Creative Commons Licence. That allows for items to be reprinted with attribution.

'Publish something in *The Conversation* and it might well end up being in the ABC or *The Guardian* or *Forbes* magazine or *Fast Company* ... you can get good traction,' he says.

Another benefit of *The Conversation* is that it highlights academics who have learned how to write in layman's terms. *The Conversation's* editors work with academics to show them how to discuss rigorous research in mainstream language in pieces about 700 words long.

Journalist Julie Hare of the *Australian Financial Review* says she uses *The Conversation* as a resource to find experts in areas she's not really sure about. 'It's the most efficient way to do that because at least you know they're open to communicating outwardly,' she says.

EXAMPLE

HITTING A NERVE

During the COVID lockdown in 2020, Debbie Haski-Leventhal drew on her past work to write an article on The Seven Positive Outcomes of COVID-19 which was published in Macquarie University's *Lighthouse*,[30] an online medium that showcases expertise and research.

'I looked at how the environment is reviving, how there is a new sense of community, how we have discovered how much we need each other and how I'm hopeful that, in the end, we will come out on the other side better humans. And it really hit a chord,' Professor Haski-Leventhal says.

The unexpected reach of the article included a teacher from Milwaukee asking if it was fine to photocopy the article and give it to her students to give them hope. An employer in South Africa wanted to share it with older employees because everyone was going through such a rough time. It was also mentioned in a newspaper in Texas and came up first when people Googled *positive outcomes of COVID*.

29 Accessed on 10 August 2021 at https://www.rednoseday.org.au/about-red-nose-day
30 https://lighthouse.mq.edu.au/

How far will your story travel?

CHAPTER 9

Learning to speak academic and journalese

- It's not dumbing down your research, it's distilling the message

- Change your writing style: tight and active, not passive voice

- Check your final research paragraph: the story lead maybe buried there

- Don't waffle. Obfuscation is a killer with media

- Check if you're communicating clearly: good preparation is the key

For academics, talking through the media requires understanding, development of skills and practise. Journalists are the mediums through which academics can reach people who may benefit from their work and expertise. But there are culture clashes.

Dumbing Down or Distillation?

Journalists can be frustrated by academics who do not speak in the language of mere mortals, whereas academics may see journalists as pandering to the great unwashed.

Part of the problem lies in a language divide between academics largely communicating with their peers, and journalists reaching diverse audiences with increasingly short attention spans.

" *I think there are different languages that people talk and learning how to speak or be bilingual in that way is a challenge.* **"**

JASON PALLANT, *SWINBURNE BUSINESS SCHOOL*

Journalists may see the precise, specialised terms which underpin academic accuracy as dull, inaccessible and unable to connect with those who consume media.

'There are some interviews I walk away from thinking there's nothing in that I can use. I mean, if you can't explain your research in layman's terms to a person on the street, you probably shouldn't be doing it,' the ABC's Conor Duffy says.

'Albert Einstein was able to communicate his ideas perfectly clearly and simply. When you're speaking to us, it's good to remember George Orwell's maxim, *never use a big word where a small one will do.*

'Most academics in Australia are doing research and teaching, so if you can distil it down enough to teach an undergrad student, it's not that much of a step further to be able to communicate it to a mass media audience,' Conor Duffy says.

You should always be thinking about the audience. And so, if you're being interviewed for expert comment, say, in an industry magazine or a newspaper, then obviously you are thinking about the audience of that publication.

" *Doing a radio interview, the same thing. You're always thinking: What do the listeners of this program or this publication want to know? But obviously, you also have to do a good job in answering the questions that the journalist is framing.* **"**

DR LIBBY SANDER, *BOND BUSINESS SCHOOL*

Marian Baird of The University of Sydney Business School says if she can explain to students the research process and outcomes, she should be able to do that to the general public. It is a skill that can be learnt, and any initial lack of confidence can be overcome with practice.

'The biggest thing is: *Have you got something to say?'* Professor Baird says.

Simplified or simplistic?

The passive, wordy style of academia is anathema to journalists, who are taught to use concise, well-targeted words that are conveyed in active tense. When there's so much information out there clamouring for attention, every word and every second of airtime counts.

Academics criticise journalists for being simplistic whereas journalists tend to see themselves as *simplifying*. Reporters know how to quickly distil key points from large amounts of information. Writing a story about a complex topic, which a 14-year-old can understand, is a highly valued professional skill.

'Anybody can write clumsily and using 100 words where 10 would probably suffice. It's a discipline to do it more cogently and concisely,' editor John Ross says.

66 *The people I like to speak to most – and there's only a few of them – are people who know the subject really well but can also express it very, very clearly and concisely in a few words. There are not many people who can do that, but they're gold.* 99

JOHN ROSS, *ASIA-PACIFIC EDITOR, TIMES HIGHER EDUCATION*

'But I suspect anybody who's capable of getting a PhD can learn these sorts of skills. Whether or not they can really engage with a camera or a crowd, I think that's a real aptitude that comes down to personality largely. But the skill of conveying it on the page, I think that's probably something that most people can do.'

The *Australian Financial Review's* Julie Hare says: 'I've spoken to scientists about some of the most obscure stuff in the universe and they can still explain it to you – that whole elevator pitch thing. Everything can be explained; you've just got to work out how to explain it.'

Stephen Matchett, Editor of *Campus Morning Mail*, says it is not so much a skill as a competency that can be relatively easily learned. 'The problem, I think, is cultural. The gap is large, but it doesn't have to be. But the way the platforms of media have changed, means that more people in academic positions need to adjust their way to suit the platforms if they want to be read outside,' he says.

FROM POMPOSITY TO CLARITY

Freya Higgins-Desbiolles of UniSA Business School came from a disadvantaged background and was the first in her family to go to university. She learned to write from doing her PhD.

'But when I learnt to write properly, what I did was learn how to write pompously,' she says. She also wanted to feel respected in academia where she had experienced a bit of imposter syndrome.

It was working on a piece in 2017 with *The Conversation* that showed her how simpler writing led to clearer ideas with which more people could engage.

At the time, Dr Higgins-Desbiolles says, she was angry because 'I put all this work into writing like a great academic and here they come and tell me to take it down to a certain level. And I really got kind of upset about that thinking, you know, *this is dumbing things down.*'

However, that work with *The Conversation* had a profound impact on her writing. 'Now I just couldn't be clearer and it comes naturally. People are not confused about what I have to say. It's really easy to read. There's a lot of academics now coming into business studies and tourism studies that are non-native English language speakers. So being clear in your English writing actually helps those guys with going through your work and thinking about your work. Clarity also supports the reading public's access to the research work.

'So I really can't thank *The Conversation* enough for helping me to do that,' she says.

Searching for a needle in a haystack of qualifications

Academic literature builds on and references previous work on complex subjects. Part of the rigour comes from considering and referencing many different views. However, those in the media often work with easily conveyed facts and more black and white opinions, which cut through the noise but may leave less room for shades of grey.

Journalists do understand why academics feel the need to say *'A' happens, except when it's a case of 'B, C or D'*. However, it's frustrating when the qualifications drown out the key points.

'It's almost a reflex feeling amongst academics that every time they lower the tone of their conversation in a way that makes sense to ordinary people, they're losing a bit of nuance,' *Times Higher Education's* John Ross says.

Ray Da Silva of UWA Business School says he has difficulty remembering the nuances in his own areas of expertise so, he wonders, how anyone else could be expected to remember the nuances in a few seconds of listening or reading.

However, he does acknowledge that academics talking about their own research are aware of the many qualifications because they are used to having every detail of their work picked up at conferences – at least in his area of accounting and finance.

But, Professor Da Silva says, with the media 'there's no need for you to add X, Y and Z. Get to the point; give them a soundbite'.

As a consumer psychologist, UQ Business School's Nicole Hartley understands the need to talk to her audience, but she finds that dealing with the media and having a chance to discuss her work is different.

'We don't think in those very concise terms, we're always thinking about how we can provide justification and rigour to every statement that we make…that's how we're trained.

'So it's hard for us to strip back and take all that out and trust that people are going to trust that we know what we're talking about,' Associate Professor Hartley says. 'We don't have to try and prove ourselves every time we open our mouths.'

Public communication often requires learning a new skill set – a lesson Nick Wailes of UNSW Business School gleaned years ago after writing a 700-word opinion piece at the request of a university media person.

The media person just 'turned it around and said *the final paragraph was actually what you should start with…and then the rest of it is unpacking and explaining it.*

'What that made pretty clear to me is that writing a journal article and being effective in the media were two very different sets of things,' Professor Wailes says.

The Australian's Tim Dodd often sees himself as a conduit to turn academic information into something that can be useful and readily understood by general readers.

He says that often means that the information is not as deep or as comprehensive as it might be in an academic paper, but the public is not going to read everything in an academic paper. You really have to look for those highlights which have more general appeal.

Dodd says a lot of academics don't really think about what a journalist is looking for and how best to express the key points they want to make. As a print journalist, he isn't too fussed when he has to dig out the interesting and useful parts of an interview. However clear messages are particularly important in broadcast interviews.

Highfalutin' words and obfuscation

When it comes to weasel words, Julie Hare, Higher Education Editor of *The Australian Financial Review* doesn't pull any punches. 'What cheeses me off the most is people who just talk in that awful bland, high umbrella kind of language that's meaningless and doesn't have anything that speaks to reality.

'I think academics use it as a point of exclusivity, that it's their little world and that you're not invited to join it. The more senior the academics, the less you get that. So it's more junior academics, who are just really kind of obviously chuffed to be a level D [academic job category] or whatever, and so they use that kind of language,' she says.

> **❝** *I can't stand the jargon and I'm never going to use those quotes where people use those truisms because it just makes me roll my eyes.* **❞**
>
> **JULIE HARE,** *AUSTRALIAN FINANCIAL REVIEW*

'If I don't understand something, I'll just keep pushing someone: *Can you explain that to me? Or can you just unpack that a bit?'* Hare says.

Journalist John Ross points out the difference between having conversations with academics, who are happy to talk off the cuff about their research, and the carefully created responses to journalist enquiries of institutions or individuals.

The latter can take two days to come back with something usually fairly brief, sometimes a lot of waffle words or a lot of dot points that don't answer your questions at all, he says.

The responses are often badly expressed filler, which may stem from the institutional culture, too many people editing the sense out of it or very deliberate waffle words to avoid saying something useful.

'It's obfuscation. Journalists become used to this sort of stuff and it just increases your suspicion levels and your scepticism,' Ross says.

Clarity is vital

Journalist Stephen Matchett says, as one voice in an infinity of media, you have to work out who you want to talk to and how to do that.

'Don't think that you should tell them what they want to hear or necessarily what interests them. It's phoney and it will show. If you've got a story, think out the best way that you can explain why it is important, but be true to yourself. That's what

PROVIDING IRRELEVANT AND UNUSABLE ANSWERS

Times Higher Education Review's Asia-Pacific Editor, John Ross, says he asked a university about how non-disparagement clause in contracts sat with academic freedom principles. In response, he received three dot points about 'how University X is so totally committed to academic freedom, blah, blah, blah, and then the fourth dot point which went to the point in my question. It just said: *These clauses are not inconsistent with our principles of academic freedom.*

Ross says the university made an assertion with no evidence and gave three dot points that were 'irrelevant and unusable'.

'If I had 5,500 words rather than 550 I could put all this waffle in, but it wouldn't be doing a service for anybody. It's a reasonable question and you'd like to get a reasonable answer, and I didn't, and that's pretty much par for the course for these sorts of questions,' he says.

I'd say to anybody in journalism be *true to yourself as to what you write and what you write about,'* he says.

Warren Hogan of UTS Business School advises being prepared to be clear for your long-term reputation and interests. 'And that's not being bold and not being opinionated. It's just being true to yourself and what you think.'

He says anyone can become muddled up talking about complex issues. 'You can really talk yourself into a bit of a tizzy, especially if you're explaining things and someone is just giving you a call out of the blue.' Not all academics are ready to talk straight off the bat to eloquently express a highly complex analytical issue. So you have just got to be careful, Professor Hogan says.

> ❝ *When I write a sentence and it's not clear, what I understand is that I don't understand the concept. So it means I need to do more thinking.* ❞
>
> **FREYA HIGGINS-DESBIOLLES,** *UniSA BUSINESS SCHOOL*

Curtin Business School's Julia Richardson questions journalists to ensure they are clear about what she is saying. Professor Richardson won't hesitate to tell them if it's not quite what she means. She says this gives journalists a sense how much flexibility they have in interpreting her information.

Is your pyramid the right way up?

For academics, it is logical to put forward a theory and then build the evidence to support the findings – in effect a pyramid structure that starts at the logical tip and works down to the base and the conclusion.

News articles are the opposite. They are written in an inverted pyramid structure with the most important material at the top. The idea is to capture the audience's attention with the headline and first paragraph so they will continue reading. By having the least important material at end of the article, a sub-editor can just cut from the bottom if the story needs to be reduced in size.

Many academics could consider having have more compelling titles and abstracts with enough punch to encourage potential readers – putting the most interesting elements of the research up front.

A checklist for communicating clearly

" It's a tough discipline to be able to distil complex ideas into a short, understandable format. "

NICK WAILES, *UNSW BUSINESS SCHOOL*

The key to clarity is preparation. Easily understood summaries and basic fact sheets can be invaluable in many forums – not just for the media – so putting in the work rarely goes to waste.

Here is our (by no means exhaustive) checklist:

Know exactly what key points you wish to make. If you are not focused, you can't expect the audience to remember your key points. Do not drown your key points under endless qualifications.

Start with why your research matters before going into specifics. Clearly convey the significance of your work (as opposed to how expert you are). If those you wish to reach do not understand why they should invest their time and attention to hear more from you, they will switch off.

Use a problem-solving structure. Discussing how your work has addressed a problem is usually a much more interesting than a chronological structure talking about logistics rather than meaning. Most people usually won't care about the minutiae of your processes.

Be simple but not simplistic. The aim is to clearly communicate to specific audiences. It takes longer to distil a concept down to its essence and provide clarity than it does to provide wordy, obtuse communications. Never confuse simplicity with being simplistic or 'dumbing it down'.

Adapt the language to suit the audience. It's fine to use specialist terms with specialist audiences, but not if you are trying to explain something to those outside that area of expertise. Therefore, avoid jargon, acronyms etc that are foreign to other people.

Ensure you are adopting the right tone to suit your audience.

Do not assume people will just know what you mean. Road test the language you are using on the those who represent the audience you want to reach. It's hard to work out what is common knowledge when you are very close to a topic.

Put numbers in context. Analogies and/or visualisations can be particularly useful to explain more detailed data. For example, few can visualise thousands of cubic metres of water, but they can visualise an Olympic swimming pool and how much water it holds.

Use sentences that contain no more than one key point. Convoluted sentences are the enemy of crisp clarity. Never underestimate the value of a full stop.

Use examples that will stick in people's minds. People are hooked into compelling stories much more than endless facts.

31 Lepore, J. 2013. *The New Economy of Letters*. The Chronicle of Higher Education. Accessed at https://www.chronicle.com/article/The-New-Economy-of-Letters/141291.

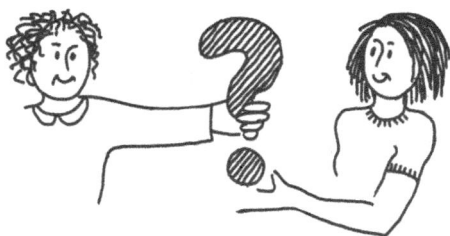

Adapt the language to suit the audience

CHAPTER 10

Attitudes to evidence

- Understand that evidence can mean different things to academics and media

- Why media may look for evidence to support a pre-determined story angle

- Avoid looking evasive and using waffle words: you'll confuse journalists

- Beware of media bias and don't be pushed into a certain point of view

Evidence-led or finding evidence to fit?

Many journalists go into academia but few, like Peter Van Onselen of Griffith and UWA Business Schools, come into journalism from academia. This may explain partly why some journalists start with a premise and seek proof to support that premise, which is very different from academics who aim to start with an open mind then follow the data and research.

'That's the big difference I've noticed in journalism and politics versus academia,' Professor Van Onselen says.

However, John Ross of *Times Higher Education* says that academics often legitimately start their research with a premise of *this is my hypothesis, this is what I'm trying to demonstrate.*

'So there are different ways that both academics and journalists can go about their business. But hopefully both groups have an open enough mind to realise and be honest with themselves if they're barking up the wrong tree,' Ross says.

The senior journalists interviewed say that reporters can look for evidence to support their premise – or story angles sought by their bosses – rather than be led by the evidence itself. But experienced practitioners, like those who specialise in areas like higher education, say they do not work that way and try to be fair, open and honest with the information in front of them. Part of the joy of their job is finding out new things.

> **"** *I like to think that that's my brand; that I'm both honest and have integrity and that I don't screw people around to get a headline.* **"**
>
> **JULIE HARE,** *AUSTRALIAN FINANCIAL REVIEW*

Nevertheless, problems can arise when less experienced reporters go into interviews to garner one specific point when they may not have a great understanding of the area under discussion.

Wrong conclusions can also be drawn by journalists trying to claw their way through potentially conflicting evidence and waffle words.

'Sometimes the institution may have reasons other than just straight-out evasiveness for using waffle words – it could just come down to culture or it could come down to internal politics. But it's this sort of evasiveness that journalists come up against constantly,' John Ross, says.

Evidence or anecdotes?

Biases inevitably creep into both academia and journalism, although Tim Dodd of *The Australian* thinks the worst enemy of journalism is over-emphasis on anecdotal evidence. For example, a story that stems from an observation about the practice in one shop, when no one has checked to see if it applies to that shop only or the whole town.

'It's up to a good journalist to find out as fast as possible if one anecdote is representative of the facts or not. That's not to say it happens all the time and often things can get through where a journalist might call up someone and the person they're talking to feels as if they're being pushed into a particular point of view. My advice is: if that happens then push back and make it clear that in your view, that's not the case,' Dodd says.

Wrong conclusions can also be drawn by journalists trying to claw their way through potentially conflicting evidence and waffle words.

CHAPTER 11

Being dropped, chopped or changed

- Why there may be a mismatch of academic and media narratives

- Yes, your information may be cut – here's why

- No, you can't review the article (maybe just your direct quotes)

- Be realistic: you won't always get attribution

- Rejection is rarely personal, so learn how to deal with it

Who controls the narrative?

Control over final stories usually rests with journalists and their editors unless there are exceptional circumstances with conditions negotiated before an interview.

Journalists write the story which is then passed on to sub-editors or others who will check and edit it to ensure the item fits with the print and/or online layout. Once the story leaves the journalist, it is largely out of the journo's hands – a point worth remembering before you berate journalists for headlines over which they have no control.

In television and radio news and current affairs, journalists (and sometimes segment or news producers) usually stay with the story throughout its creation. They will script and edit their own material or work with a professional video editor before someone more senior approves the story.

The standard of fact-checking and editing in media organisations can vary enormously. The most rigorous organisations may have two or three people between the journalist and the readers, listeners or viewers. In other organisations there may be no filters between what the journalist writes and the public. Where once you had sub-editors who were experts in fields such as sport, now there are more pools of sub-editors covering all areas. These sub-editors may edit an economics story one minute and a local council story the next.

Stories updated frequently online may become increasingly accurate as more information is received.

Narratives of academics and journalists rarely match and it can be disappointing to find that information you've supplied, or large slabs of your interview, have been cut.

Tim Dodd of *The Australian* says not everyone interviewed will end up in the story. 'It might be because someone else gave you a quote that you think is more pertinent and more clear and more usable. It might be because you just spoke to a lot of people in the course of this and there's no room for them in the story or it might be that the journalist actually wrote you into the story but the story was cut in the editing process and that particular part was left out. There's all sorts of reasons why it might happen.'

" The journalists' role is usually to question and interrogate and use our research to suit their purposes. So you have to be a bit careful and you don't have complete control over your own research once it gets into the journalist's hands.

MARIAN BAIRD, *UNIVERSITY OF SYDNEY BUSINESS SCHOOL* **"**

UNSW's Richard Holden says it is important to understand that it's just part of the journalistic process and, at the end of the day, it's their story, not your story.

Macquarie Business School's Elizabeth Sheedy says she relies on journalists to present her views fairly unless she is writing an opinion piece over which she has control.

Professor Sheedy says it's important to become comfortable with journalists not allowing you to review their articles before publication, although she's had no problem with being allowed to review her direct quotes.

If a journalist does agree to send you your quotes for the article, it's good form to respond very quickly and not hold up the news production process.

Frustration with lack of attribution

Most journalists add links to research and other articles – something that is good for academic and media credibility. However, it may stick in the craw when a journalist paraphrases, without credit, an academic's expert knowledge. That flies in the face of academic standards around referencing contributions to one's work.

Journalist John Ross understands the frustration of academics who have a long conversation that leads to only a short quote.

He says it may be 20 minutes into a conversation before he will hear the quote he wants, which is a short statement that adds something really important to the story.

He always tries to include a person's name in his story, as it is fair to the academic and shows he has spoken to an expert and is not just editorialising. He is also keen on including links to relevant papers.

Campus Morning Mail Editor, Stephen Matchett, says if a journalist phones to talk to you about a specific subject and does the interview on the spot, then the journalist 'has a broader obligation to ensure that the story is full and covers everything'.

But if a journalist asks an academic to write 1000 words on a topic by the next morning then doesn't run it, it could be due to two reasons:

'One, the copy just wasn't good enough in which case, the journalist should have gone back and said: *Look, it's not there. It needs this, this, this, and this. Why don't I rewrite the lead for you and see what you think?*

'Or they say: *Sorry. The Archduke Franz Ferdinand was assassinated overnight. They had to tear down the op-ed page*'. (He does point out that the dropping of an op-ed page is less likely now that online op-eds can, theoretically, run forever).

Dealing with rejection

Carl Rhodes of UTS Business School says academics are well-schooled in being rejected for academic journals and promotions.

For him, being proactive can become difficult when he writes about something on the same day it is happening in the news, but the media outlet does not reject it until a couple of days later when it is no longer newsworthy.

'You may have lost your opportunity,' he says. 'It can be disappointing, but you just have to keep on keeping on. It is par for the course and also depends on where you are pitching.'

Curtin Business School's Steven Rowley says: 'You can't take anything personally, really. They're just trying to do their job. It's quite often you'll get a phone call or email saying *can you do this now?* When you email back in maybe 20 minutes, you won't hear back because they have found somebody else. It happens all the time; just fishing around for somebody.'

If UWA's Raymond Da Silva has no response to a piece he has written he will follow up his initial email and then, if the article is not accepted, offer it elsewhere.

Journalists rarely say *'no, it's not good enough'* to a piece. 'They'll say *this won't work for now for us, but thank you,'* Professor Da Silva says.

His takeaway? 'You're not as important and your views are not the be all and end all of life. But it takes some time to learn that lesson.'

❝ *To know that you're not the centre of the universe. It's a really good lesson.* **❞**

MARIAN BAIRD, *UNIVERSITY OF SYDNEY BUSINESS SCHOOL*

It's worth learning to become more comfortable with journalists

CHAPTER 12

Is investing your time in media work worth it?

- Build your media engagement – it may prompt new research ideas

- Make a habit of prioritising media requests whenever you can

- Familiarity breeds...more efficient and beneficial media relationships

- Tip: suggest journalists email you their questions if there's time

- Your TV audience may be a million people, plus online and social media

How much time an academic chooses, or is able, to devote to working with the media involves prioritising your time, and your choice of media and media outlets.

UNSW Business School's Frederik Anseel says those who focus on global reputations and academic careers, which still depend largely on publication in academic journals, may not be interested in investing time with domestic journalists.

However, Professor Anseel sees media work as integral to the research cycle. 'Often my research comes from engaging with journalistic businesses. You get ideas, you conduct research, you have the results, and then you want to communicate and receive feedback and that gives you new ideas.'

Michael Callaghan of Deakin Business School says it is very hard to find the time because talking to a journalist invariably means moving another task to another time.

However, he says, academics live and work in a very privileged world in which a lot of work, other than teaching and meetings, can be shifted around to accommodate media requests.

❝ *Prioritising it is what you need to do to get your name and your work and your research out there.* **❞**

MICHAEL CALLAGHAN, *DEAKIN BUSINESS SCHOOL*

Relationships helping to lessen the load

Ongoing relationships with journalists can lessen the amount of time required for an interview. 'Sometimes it will just be a 15-minute conversation because they know how to talk to me. They can tell me what they're after and I tell them what I think and the job's done,' Dr Callaghan says.

Louise Grimmer from UTAS Business School enjoys media work but can find it hard to meet all interview requests. Her quick alternative is for journalists to email her questions so she can respond with quotes. 'I know they're on deadline and they know how I work,' she says.

Time-consuming television

Television can be one of the greatest time consumers.

The camera crew needs to set up, sometimes at more than one location. Your interview may be stopped and started by innumerable noises only a microphone can pick up. They may want to film a sit-down interview and then other material while you are walking and talking through a wireless microphone.

If there's any filming of action, the odds are the camera operator will, for editing purposes, want to shoot the same action from several angles. And they are just a few of the many distractions and interruptions that can waylay the best of plans.

There are skilled media performers who will leave the camera crew to set up and, when the journalist or camera operator says they are ready, the interviewee will come in, answer a few quick questions and be out of there in a jiffy.

However, if you have never worked with pre-recorded or live television before, it's wise to double or triple the amount of time you expect the filming to take.

Television interviews can 'take an awful lot of time and more often than not, it will be – if you're really lucky – a five-second, 15-second grab' from a 90-minute investment of your time, Dr Callaghan says.

Louise Grimmer from UTAS Business School says her first experience of being interviewed live on a morning television show was 'excruciating'.

'The amount of research that their research assistant had done was unlike anything I've ever seen in my life, and the segment went for about two minutes. It was eye opening: the amount of work that goes into live television that just doesn't then get broadcast,' Dr Grimmer says.

Whether the interview was worth your time may depend on the viewership of the TV news or current affairs show, which can be around a million people in Australia. And that doesn't count the pre-show promotions as well as the online and social media replays of all or part of the story after a program has aired.

Television can become one of the greatest time consumers.

3

Working with journalists

CHAPTER 13

Building and maintaining media relationships

- How media gather information for their stories

- Building your media relationships: advice from experts

- Respect: remember it's a two-way street

- Don't 'cultivate': no one wants to be used

- Focus on your relevant media outlets

" Media is very much a relationships business. "

ELIZABETH SHEEDY, *MACQUARIE BUSINESS SCHOOL*

Relationships with journalists can be purely transactional. One-off contact. Job done. No follow up.

For example, you or your institution may distribute a media release or a media alert offering you an as expert for comment on a new report or upcoming event. A journalist then calls you for more information and over-the-phone quotes or may organise a time for a video interview in person. The journalist's story is published in one or several media and that's that.

For a journalist that is Story Gathering 101. Sometimes a shortage of reporters, time and/or lack of inclination to put in some work results in slabs of a media release being used by a media outlet without even a change in wording. Within the ranks of more diligent journalists there is criticism of this so-called 'handout mentality' and the number of stories from re-written media releases.

However, for spin doctors, that's a good scenario: they write the media release so it reads like a news story and it's used the way they want, sometimes with the added bonus of still images or video excerpts supplied by the spin doctor/PR company/ communications team. (Although public relations experts have been known to complain that 'bloody journos want us to write everything for them. They even want us to line up the talent').

The media release is geared towards a traditional model of pushing information out to the world, with the journalist and media outlets as recipients who broadcast or publish to a wide audience.

However building your community, which is more in keeping with today's social media model, is likely to lead to deeper relationships with journalists that can last for decades. Those relationships may start as fleeting encounters but, with nurturing on both sides and development of mutually beneficial stories, they can grow into valuable professional connections.

Building symbiotic relationships

" Treat journalists as partners in the process, not the enemy. You are the expert – they need you for the story but can help get your message out. "

TIM HARCOURT, *UNSW BUSINESS SCHOOL*

With a healthy relationship, an academic can benefit from having a trusted and respected journalist who can help to translate information for more mainstream audiences, reach people beyond the academic's niche, often provide sound media advice and give greater context to issues being debated in newsrooms and the wider public.

The upside for the journalist is having a trusted, very accessible, authentic source of expert opinion, credible information and perspectives, rigorous research and reliability, along with the ability to communicate well in language the public can understand.

Deakin Business School's Michael Callaghan says journalists often need to show they have covered both sides of a story so it can be efficient to contact an authoritative source.

" My attitude has always been, if a reporter rings me, I'll pick up the phone. If it is in an area where I feel I can give an informed opinion, then I'm more than happy to provide an informed opinion. "

MICHAEL CALLAGHAN, *DEAKIN BUSINESS SCHOOL*

Dr Callaghan follows up with reporters after initial encounters then connects and communicates with them on social media, so his network builds over time. It may be a couple of years before something related to his expertise arises again, but being connected makes it more likely that the journalist will call him when it does.

'The more you get out there, the more likely journalists will come back to you. The more industry is aware of what you're doing, the more potential there is for future partnerships, and the easier it is to disseminate future research findings. So in many ways, it's a very symbiotic relationship,' Curtin Business School's Steven Rowley says.

Marian Baird of The University of Sydney Business School says it's important to ensure each journalist is clear on the points she is trying to impart. 'After a while, you have enough confidence and enough of a relationship that builds up that they respect you. So I have the same journalists talking to me now, 10 years later.'

❝ It comes down to hard work, talking to people. Relationship building is key. ❞

CONOR DUFFY, *AUSTRALIAN BROADCASTING CORPORATION*

On the downside, Professor Kristy Muir points out that the precarious nature of journalism over the past few years has made it more difficult to build relationships. 'Some of the most fabulous journalists have been lost from previously strong publications and institutions. So much of it is freelance now, which means that it's much harder to get a steady relationship.'

The ABC's Senior Business Correspondent, Peter Ryan says: 'A really paramount thing, that I think a lot of reporters don't really get, is that you have to spend a lot of time building up those relationships at different levels. I have the measure that   if you put a call through and someone rings you back, particularly if it's in the evening or in the early morning, that's a pretty good sign. But you just have to be able to work that.'

Creating professional respect

Journalist Conor Duffy says respect and understanding are key.

'Being respectful, being in contact, being available, maybe sometimes helping journalists with stories that they're working on, where it might not be an obvious benefit to you – like connecting people with someone they need. Those kinds of things really create a lot of professional respect.'

Duffy is no fan of academics who think 'they are the sun around which the universe orbits. I'm much less likely to spend time taking their call, or even speaking to them, because I have probably at least a hundred pitches every week plus my own stories that I'm generating'.

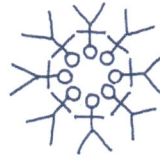

Louise Grimmer of UTAS Business School respects journalists' time by always being careful to let them know what she is doing – even when she is unable to talk – so they are not left waiting to hear back from her.

Can you cultivate a journalist or vice versa?

The question of how to 'cultivate' journalists often comes up in media training sessions. The advice? Start by moving away from the idea of 'cultivating' a person to focus on building a really professional relationship.

No one wants to feel like a tool to be used by someone else – no matter whether they are a journalist or a 'source'.

" *If a journalist had a feeling he was being cultivated he'd probably run a million miles.* **"**

CONOR DUFFY, *AUSTRALIAN BROADCASTING CORPORATION*

STARTING TO BUILD A NETWORK

Michael Callaghan of Deakin Business School started doing media because it was put in his performance review. He was particularly nervous and thought it was a hard ask.

'My attitude was: *I'm an academic. Why are you asking me to be a media tart?* Once I had done two or three…I worked out that it was actually enjoyable. It wasn't that hard. I kept in contact with those reporters and I very quickly came to the conclusion that if you want to be able to have the medium to get a story out of your own research, the easiest way to do that is to have a group of reporters you've dealt with in the past. Now, it's not a network that you should ever exploit, because very quickly they work out you are using them rather than the other way around.'

They also want to feel like you have done the most basic homework.

'Know whom it is you're talking to, know what they're interested in, get their name right and know the issues that they cover,' advises the ABC's Peter Ryan.

Because of the configuration of ABC emails that start with surnames, Peter has received communications saying: 'Hi Ryan. I hope you're having a wonderful day. I just wanted to reach out to see if…' He says he doesn't worry too much about the 'Ryan' bit but, if you have ever listened to him on ABC Radio or seen him on ABC TV, you would know his name is Peter.

The flip side is journalists who do not accurately describe academic affiliations. Steven Rowley of Curtin Business School finds it frustrating when journalists come up with many different ways to describe where he is from. They can make him feel that 'they don't really care who they're speaking to; they just want some random academic to try and provide some sort of gravitas behind the story'.

However, he doesn't take it personally. 'I'm doing them a favour but it's part of my job and it's also important for me to raise my profile.'

Small things count

Like all professionals, journalists appreciate it when someone bothers to provide thoughtful commentary on their work while expecting nothing in return. A comment online, through social media, or direct email can help build relationships. You can also help boost engagement and show them you are tracking what journalists are doing by following them and re-tweeting posts on Twitter and other social media platforms.

Another small but important point is how rarely people thank journalists for producing great stories that benefit those involved and vice versa.

A famous old journalist told Conor Duffy that it's not rocket science, it's just those basic little human touches that people appreciate.

It goes both ways. 'We need to obviously express our thanks when someone moves heaven and earth to arrange access for us. When relationships are good and there's flow back and forth like that, people are more likely to help each other out on short notice,' Duffy says.

They are also more likely to trust the journalist to deal fairly when times are rough.

'Certainly, there's been some universities where I've done some stories that they really didn't like, but we were still able to have a very productive relationship because there was trust and it was very straightforward about how the story was going to proceed,' he says.

DEVELOPED RELATIONSHIPS COMING INTO PLAY

In 2017, the ABC's Peter Ryan won a coveted Walkley Award for Coverage of a Major News Event or Issue.

At the time, the Walkley judges said:[32]

'The extent of the Commonwealth Bank crisis exposed by the ABC's Peter Ryan was all but unfathomable:[33] 53,700 separate AUSTRAC breaches of anti-money laundering and terrorism financing laws, as a consequence of allegations that the CBA allowed money launderers and crime groups to exploit the bank's intelligent deposit machines. The potential fine for each individual offence is a maximum of $18 million.

'Ryan not only broke the story but provided extensive coverage and comprehensive analysis across all ABC platforms in the months subsequent, including the first broadcast interview with the Commonwealth Bank's chief executive Ian Narev.'

Peter Ryan says he broke the story on a Thursday, there was a crisis on the Friday and over the weekend, then he discovered CBA was doing a briefing for a few print journos on Sunday.

Ryan says: 'I phoned up their corporate affairs person and said: *What the F's going on? I should be on this. The CBA person said: Ah, the lawyers have advised us not to do any broadcast interviews. And I said: Well, I think that you need to tell the lawyers that this is a pretty important story. I broke the story and also it's important that you get out on the front foot. And I'm only going to need him for five minutes.'*

After much to-ing and fro-ing CBA agreed to the interview on the condition Ian Narev was live on ABC Radio's AM show.

With limited time on air, Ryan homed in on four key questions: How did this happen? What are you doing about it? What happens next? And when are you resigning?

Ryan says pushing hard for the broadcast interview was vital, but his professional relationship with the Commonwealth Bank also played an important part.

'In their dealings with me they were always, in general, upfront and honest and made people available. And at the same time, I felt that I was always regarded as being upfront, no tricks, honest. I would do the right thing, but would ask the hard questions, but hopefully do that in a courteous way, than the other way around,' he says.

Relevant outlets

Elizabeth Sheedy of Macquarie Business School has developed relationships with journalists who cover banking and finance – the industry most relevant to her work.

'The advantage is that quite often, when a big story comes up, they'll approach me for comment or I can send an email and say: *Are you writing a story on this?* Or perhaps a first story has already come out and you can say: *Are you planning on any follow up story, because I've got a few things I could say on that?*' Professor Sheedy says.

The University of Sydney Business School's Rae Cooper identifies journalists who are particularly interested in her area. 'I'm really happy to give them data and give them exclusives because they're interested in my work and I'm interested in their stories going well, and they'll get the stories out. So it's a great symbiotic relationship.'

Warren Hogan of UTS Business School also sees the positives in helping journalists by providing background that can improve their expertise. He says good journalists have a critical and challenging role that involves being on top of a lot of issues. Good journalists also want to hear different views.

During his banking career, Professor Hogan used to have lunches with a couple of journalists and people from his banking team. It was a more intimate way of getting to know journalists and build up a level of comfort, which required only the investment of time and the cost of lunch.

Frederik Anseel worked closely with journalists in Europe before he joined UNSW Business School. Whenever he had a scoop or something new, he would send it to a journalist with whom he had a good connection. The offer was exclusive access to the research results if the journalist did a story. 'And, of course, journalists like this much better,' Professor Anseel says. 'If you just send out a public press release, everyone has the same information. There's no value for them.'

Being approached frequently by media also led to Professor Anseel being asked to write a bi-weekly column for a financial newspaper in Belgium. Three years on, he is still writing that column.

32 Accessed on 1/9/21 at https://www.walkleys.com/award-winners/peter-ryan-major-news-event/
33 "Breaking News – CBA risks massive fines over anti-money laundering & terrorism financing law breaches; CBA chief executive Ian Narev in first broadcast interview re scandal – tells Peter Ryan "mistakes were made" but not resigning; CBA cuts Ian Narev's bonus to "zero" as a result of Austrac money laundering allegations"
"ASIC to investigate CBA disclosure to stock exchange. When did it know about money-laundering risks?"
" Ian Narev to retire by 30 June 2016 as CBA chief executive; APRA announces independent inquiry into CBA"

*A small but important point is
how rarely people thank journalists
for producing great stories that benefit
those involved and vice versa.*

CHAPTER 14

What journalists want from you

- Two different tasks: giving comments and writing opinion pieces

- What makes you a go-to academic?

- How to be ready when you're needed

- Do media play favourites?

- How to become a fresh voice for media

“ *Academics are so important. They cut through the spin. They give expert advice. Their research is evidence based. The media need and want that.* **”**

CATHERINE WEBBER, *BOND UNIVERSITY*

Richard Holden of UNSW says there are two aspects to working with journalists: being called for comment on a particular issue and generating your own opinion pieces.

The former may involve a journalist writing about issues such as interest rates, tax policy or housing policy. 'They want a comment from such and such an academic at such and such an institution. For that, I definitely have built relationships with journalists. That's something that's happened relatively organically over time,' Professor Holden says.

He now knows a few journalists who often text and ask if he is interested in commenting on a story they are writing or if he can help them think through an issue.

When it comes to opinion pieces, Professor Holden recommends building relationships with the opinion page editors of major media outlets by writing interesting op-eds in a timely manner.

“ *The perceived neutrality of academics helps journalists because it's not a paid-for comment. It's not a press release. It's not coming from a PR company. It's somebody who has some knowledge of the area.* **”**

STEVE WORTHINGTON, *SWINBURNE BUSINESS SCHOOL*

ABC Business Correspondent Peter Ryan finds academic perspectives useful, particularly when chief executives or politicians are 'pretty much talking their book'.

He cites the example of the Banking Royal Commission, during which he would talk to experts such as Elizabeth Sheedy from Macquarie Business School about corporate governance and other issues.[34]

'So, you might have the actual story going on but have a third party to put something in particular context or to offer commentary,' Ryan says. He also may talk to academics when they have interesting research or reports to share.

The Higher Education Editor of *The Australian*, Tim Dodd, has two reasons to interview academics:

1. For a story about the specialty area in which the academic is involved
2. When writing a story about higher education in general and they have a useful view about the way their university or the higher education system works.

What makes a person good talent or that go-to academic?

❝ *Familiarity, authenticity, knowing the subject, speaking honestly, not saying bullshit.* ❞

JOHN ROSS, *ASIA-PACIFIC EDITOR, TIMES HIGHER EDUCATION*

❝ *Being talented and demonstrative…You've got to be curious, and then you've got to have the passion to communicate that curiosity to others.* ❞

STEPHEN MATCHETT, *EDITOR, CAMPUS MORNING MAIL*

The Australian's Tim Dodd says journalists go back to people they think have good information and insights; people with a handle on what is going on in their work or field and are prepared to share that.

Nick Wailes of UNSW adds that, while your subject matter is important, responsiveness is also key. Even being the best in a field won't attract journalists if you don't get back to them.

This can work both ways. It can be extremely frustrating to deal with journalists who are arrogant and/or never respond to story suggestions or commentary offered. However, it is worth noting the significant difference between offering a journalist carefully considered pieces which consider the journalist's interests, as opposed to spamming them with endless media releases that are sent to everyone. The latter do not require a response.

So do the media play favourites?

Deakin Business School's Michael Callaghan maintains that media outlets do have favourites who are trotted out frequently. Those favourites make the time to talk to the media, which is particularly important if academics want to show their expertise and areas of research. They can also be available to assist journalists in verifying the accuracy of information.

"Journalists want to work with people who they know are generally available and who are able to translate their message in an accessible way. It's really important to be professional and to obviously do a great job in the moment."

LIBBY SANDER, *BOND BUSINESS SCHOOL*

Macquarie Business School's Debbie Haski-Leventhal focuses on tapping into what journalists are looking for. This means utilising research, knowledge and intellect to appeal to the general public and show the connection to current interests of the wider public.

Bond University's Catherine Webber – a former newspaper editor – says being available and reliable is hugely important, especially when fewer resources and the 24/7 news cycle put more pressure on journalists.

She says it can be tough for time-stretched journalists to find the expert in the field and wait to see if the expert gets back and agrees to talk. 'I don't think they just favour certain academics for the sake of favouring them. I think it's just they're on the phone. They can get them. It's easy. You know, they've performed before.'

Marian Baird of The University of Sydney Business School learned very quickly that once a journalist finds someone who is willing to talk and has done some research, they will come back to ask about a subject that is similar.

Steve Worthington of Swinburne Business School has long-standing relationships with a few journalists, but finds a lot of changes in the media and reporters' names which suddenly appear and disappear. He tries to help journalists where he can and appreciates being seen as someone worth contacting in the future.

Journalists 'won't overuse you because then it becomes boring for everybody', Professor Worthington says.

Curtin Business School's Steven Rowley has certain journalists who come back to him repeatedly. However, he has noticed that if an academic has a bad time with a journalist, the journalist will go to someone else.

Journalists 'are a fickle bunch but they will latch on to the person they know they can go to who'll respond quickly and they can use a few lines in their story', Professor Rowley says.

Saying yes and switching into top gear

QUT Business School's Gary Mortimer will get a phone call from a news journalist saying something like: *Listen, can you do a couple of grabs? We can come down to your office now or to your house.* Professor Mortimer then needs to be ready 'to rock and roll in 30 minutes' – something he says any academics who know their stuff can do.

Swinburne's Jason Pallant contends that saying *yes* and doing it quickly have been the biggest predictors of whether journalists will come back to him.

'If you want to be the go-to person, you've got to be willing to get a phone call at 7.45am because at 8.15am they need a spot on the radio filled and they want an immediate comment on that morning's news. So you need to be quick at responding, quick at saying *yes* and formulating a view you can share.'

However, Dr Pallant points out that rapid response news commentary may not appeal to some academics because there is little room for deep analysis or thought when providing two sentences for an online news article or a 15-second grab for a two-minute video news story.

Journalist Tim Dodd agrees that translating academic information into a form readily understood by a general audience means the information is not as deep or as comprehensive as it might be in an academic paper.

'But the public is not going to read everything in an academic paper. You really have to look for those highlights which have more general appeal and hopefully which are useful as well,' Dodd says.

Finding fresh voices

Journalists are almost always on the lookout for fresh voices. A good example of this is the ever-widening number of epidemiologists and other public health professionals interviewed as the COVID-19 pandemic progressed.

John Ross of *Times Higher Education* says he is always looking to widen the net of people, and sometimes finds someone new who can help to create a meaningful story in 550 words. 'This is somebody I want to speak to again because this person has an informed, fresh and useful view for the sector.'

34 *The Australian Royal Commission into Misconduct in the Banking, Superannuation and Financial Services Industry* started in 2017. The final report was handed down in 2019.

CHAPTER 15

Are you expert enough?

- What makes an expert in the media?

- Do you discuss others' research?

- Differentiate between research and informed comment

- When should you say no?

Expert on research vs expert in discipline

Several academics identified the tension between talking about their own research compared to talking more widely as an expert.

Part of that could be due to the academic training, which emphasises rigor and discussing only areas you understand deeply. There can also be a sense of encroaching on another's territory or being fearful of not speaking with pinpoint accuracy.

Bond University's Catherine Webber says there are times when an academic may think he or she should have been the one contacted by the media because they are THE expert on a topic. However, she counsels that it is more productive to think: *What can I offer that says something different?*

Webber maintains media coverage should not be a competition between academics: it is about adding your voice, even when you disagree with others. 'That's public life. We need to discuss and throw around ideas and agree to disagree or not,' she says.

So when do you become an expert?

When Gary Mortimer of QUT Business School finished his PhD and started in academia, he struggled with the concept of being an expert. It wasn't until ABC Radio wanted to talk about him about his research and retail expertise, that he began to rethink his view of being 'just an old retailer who did a PhD.'

Professor Mortimer points out that academics becomes experts in their PhD areas of research. The challenge is to then build the confidence to own that space. It took years before he was comfortable commenting publicly when he disagreed with something said by a CEO of a major company.

Libby Sander of Bond University thinks the required expertise is probably something that grows naturally from writing about new research in an industry piece or in *The Conversation*. 'Then it starts to evolve because the more experience you get as a researcher, then obviously you have more of a feel about how your findings relate to various areas.'

Providing informed opinions

Michael Callaghan of Deakin Business School considers it part of his duty to provide an informed opinion based on his understanding of strategic marketing, business strategy, ethics and corporate social responsibility. Therefore, he will comment on how an organisation's performance compares with best practice even when he has not researched the specific organisation under discussion. However many academics won't do that, creating problems for a journalist who needs informed experts to verify accuracy and provide a perspective on the story.

Macquarie University's Elizabeth Sheedy makes it clear when her opinion pieces are based on explicit research findings or are informed comment. 'I guess there is that danger that the lines could be blurred – I do make an effort to try and be clear about that. Journalists aren't always good at noting the difference but you can't control every element of what appears in the media.'

Richard Holden of UNSW Business School acknowledges the dangers of being seen as 'a talking head' – something he tries to avoid because he 'got into this racket to do serious academic research and that's still my passion and my primary role.'

There is a balance between talking solely about your own research and talking about everything. Professor Holden says he uses a tool kit, based on first principles from his basic training, that equips him to talk on a broader range of issues. His popular communications reflect his economic perspective that considers, for example, 'how someone who believes in some combination of markets, but also fairness, might think about an issue'.

So when should you pass up a great opportunity?

Sarah Jane Kelly of UQ Business School thinks if you're newsworthy enough to make prime time or a major news platform, then you should take that opportunity. If you are asked to do an interview outside your area, she advises keeping your reputation intact. This may mean declining the interview, finding someone else more suitable to do it and giving that person a leg up through your recommendation.

" Don't ever get yourself into a situation where you're making a comment on something you don't know anything about or you don't know if it's true. "

LIBBY SANDER, *BOND BUSINESS SCHOOL*

Julie Hare of *The Australian Financial Review* says it's fine if an interviewee does not want to answer a question because it's not in their field of research. She is happy to be pointed in another direction.

If academics are worried about straying into areas in which they are not completely comfortable or sure of their facts, they can always have a caveat on the conversation. Journalist John Ross says this could be: '*This is what I think, but I'd rather double check it before you publish it.*'

'It's a very reasonable conversation to have and most journalists will respect that. If they don't, they'll probably say so. The only reservation most journalists would have is the time that might be involved because they're on deadline,' he says.

Journalists talk about other people's work all the time

Journalists are (or should be) well versed in the unacceptability of plagiarism and copyright infringement but, when it comes to the well-embedded academic sense of ownership around specific work, the media operates very differently.

'We talk about other people's work all the time. We try and translate ideas or views or opinions or assertions into a form that you can spread around to an audience and be understood. So we have no inhibitions about explaining to a more general audience what other people have worked on,' Higher Education Editor of *The Australian*, Tim Dodd, says.

Researchers need not get to the point where they're happy to talk about what others have done as well as their own work but should not say *another researcher has done this or there is a view of that*. Instead use verbal citations that specify who has done what.

John Ross says a verbal citation gives him options. 'It's directing me as a journalist to an area that I really should be looking at for answers. I can either cite the approximate citation from the person I've been speaking to or go to the original source and look for that. It gives me choices and the world is slightly better informed as a result, I suspect.'

And then there's the all-about-me crowd

There is a coterie of academics who have transcended individual institutions, commoditised their expertise and become global celebrities.

However, much more common are 'academic starlets', contends Peter Fleming of UTS in his book *Dark Academia.*[35]

Professor Fleming says starlets 'cultivate brand recognition to advance their careers within academia'. Unlike distinguished professors they will aggressively manage their public profiles and 'shamelessly' build social networks, media contacts and connections. They will give interviews and opinions on any topic because being seen is more important than the ideas being put forward.

He says famous academics can leverage their reputation to obtain higher-paying positions at more prestigious universities where 'they automatically publicise the institution, like walking billboards.'

Anyone you know who fits that bill?

35 Fleming, P. 2021, *Dark Academia: How Universities Die*, Pluto Press, London.

CHAPTER 16

Journalistic ethics is not an oxymoron

- Why you should check journalists' credentials

- Be wary of journalists with an agenda

- Avoiding the 'gotcha' interviews

- Where journalism integrity could be improved

- Yes, there is a Journalist Code of Ethics

Many years ago, when this author was conducting an ethics lecture for final-year undergraduate journalism students, students responded to a series of hypothetical situations.

With time for careful consideration and the weighing of options available, the group was largely in agreement about how different scenarios should be handled in ethical ways.

They were then put under extreme time pressure to see how their responses might differ. One by one, I related real situations encountered as a TV reporter on the road and gave the students 15 seconds or less to make a decision. For example, one of the scenes involved a clearly traumatised girl physically attacking our cameraman who, for public interest purposes, was filming in the middle of an evacuation centre during a major bushfire.

Within half an hour, the differences between the students became apparent. At one end of the spectrum were those who would clearly do anything to get a good story, with the end justifying the means. At the other were the altruists who, without a degree of toughening up, an increase in scepticism and a more realistic view of the world beyond their bubble, seemed less likely to become incisive and insightful journalists. Most of the class landed somewhere in the middle.

We all know how easy it is to be Monday morning quarterbacks and critique efforts in hindsight. The media do it to high-profile figures all the time. But journalists are frequently in situations that provide little time for debate of ethical pros and cons. So while most journalists strive to be as fair as possible, context is often important.

No formal accreditation

With no professional accreditation, anyone can call themselves a journalist. This means it is wise to look at journalists' track records when judging the cut of their jibs.

Industry oversight

There are bodies that oversee journalists – the Australian Press Council and the Australian Communications and Media Authority – but they are often criticised for being toothless tigers.

There is also a journalist Code of Ethics[36], that applies to members of the journalists' union, the Media Entertainment and Arts Alliance. The Code calls on journalists to commit to honesty, fairness, independence and respect for the rights of others. (See the full Code on page 136)

In a recent webinar run by the Walkley Foundation, which awards the most prestigious national journalism accolades, the lack of industry policing was highlighted as a major issue on the panel *Improving the Integrity and Accountability of Journalism in Australia*.[37]

Not one of the four panel journalists rated journalism ethics today any higher than 5 out of 10, with Peter Greste of the Alliance for Journalists' Freedom giving a paltry 3.5 out of 10.

❝ *There is a lot of journalism-like content out there that isn't produced to a rigorous standard or subject to a compliance procedure.* ❞

PETER GRESTE, *ALLIANCE FOR JOURNALISTS' FREEDOM*

❝ *We need to stop making it about us and make it about the audience…put the journalism and audience at the forefront again.* ❞

SAFFRON BOWDEN, *AUSTRALIAN COMMUNITY MEDIA*

The panel raised the issues of:

- The blurring of lines between opinion, analysis and reportage
- Hyper-partisanship in Australian media
- Journalists serving media owners and pay cheques
- Journalists who are mouthpieces for vested interests, as opposed to being fearlessly independent
- The rise of celebrity journalists, where the journalist is too often the story
- A disconnect between newsrooms and their audiences, especially as increased pressure on newsrooms allows less time for journalists to be in the community where they are directly accountable for what they write
- Journalists using their social media feeds very differently from the rest of their professional practice, which involves professional standards such as fact-checking
- Fierce competition between media organisations skewing standards
- Journalists needing to pay more attention to what audiences want, including less salacious material.

Fair, objective or following agendas?

The Editor of the *Campus Morning Mail*, Stephen Matchett, says the job of journalists is 'to make a call on what is important and what matters, and to report it'. There are some journalists with whom you should be cautious but 'the vast, vast, vast majority of them will report you fairly'.

Matchett is concerned about journalists who pursue agendas and says that you can be 'rock-solid sure' that certain journalists will approach stories from angles that suit their own values and the values of the people they believe are their audience. In contrast, he hopes you could read *Campus Morning Mail* from one year to the next and not have any idea of his personal affiliations.

The *Australian Financial Review's* Julie Hare says some academics may be media shy for a reason and it is up to trustworthy, experienced journalists to prove they will not be badly done by.

The ABC's Conor Duffy agrees that most journalists try to be fair and objective. 'I guess the basic rules are around right of reply, always trying to get both sides of the story and giving people the proper amount of time to enable that to happen rather than just hitting them with a really difficult request half an hour before deadline. The cultures in the different newsrooms in Australia partly inform how the journalist is going to act,' Duffy says.

Bad behaviour includes 'calling you literally half an hour before deadline and saying: *We're going to smash you up tomorrow. You've got 30 minutes to give us a response* and the front page or the TV story's already written. It's just an arse-covering exercise (if I can use that word),' Duffy says.

He outlines a much more ethical approach would be a journalist who may be 'doing a difficult topic that you would probably prefer wasn't canvassed in the media, but they're making a genuine attempt to include your perspective and come to you with something that's challenging'.

Academics have said they have experienced 'gotcha' moments when the journalist has deliberately led them into saying something they would prefer not to have said. Others have journalists and/or media outlets with whom one encounter was one too many. But these instances are definitely infrequent.

Not always what you expect

It can be wise to look well beyond your perception of a media platform. There are likely to be ethically challenged journalists as well as highly reputable ones. It can also be useful to look harder at how the outlet reports issues of interest to you. It may be that the promotion of a story, or a headline written by someone other than the journalist, is sensationalist but the actual story is not.

QUT's Gary Mortimer says he used to be wary of a nightly current affairs show because of its tabloid style reportage. 'But I've worked with them on many occasions and I actually find them to be really good now and again.'

Professor Mortimer also points out it is in journalists' interests not to burn bridges and lose access to people they may want to include in stories.

36 https://www.meaa.org/meaa-media/code-of-ethics/
37 Walkley Foundation. 2021. *A Better of Trust: Improving the Integrity and Accountability of Journalism in Australia.* Accessed on 7 September 2021 at https://www.youtube.com/watch?v=604oiVPpJiY.

MEAA JOURNALIST CODE OF ETHICS

Journalists will educate themselves about ethics and apply the following standards:

1 2 3 4 5 6 7 8 9 10 11 12

1. Report and interpret honestly, striving for accuracy, fairness and disclosure of all essential facts. Do not suppress relevant available facts, or give distorting emphasis. Do your utmost to give a fair opportunity for reply.

2. Do not place unnecessary emphasis on personal characteristics, including race, ethnicity, nationality, gender, age, sexual orientation, family relationships, religious belief, or physical or intellectual disability.

3. Aim to attribute information to its source. Where a source seeks anonymity, do not agree without first considering the source's motives and any alternative attributable source. Where confidences are accepted, respect them in all circumstances.

4. Do not allow personal interest, or any belief, commitment, payment, gift or benefit, to undermine your accuracy, fairness or independence.

5. Disclose conflicts of interest that affect, or could be seen to affect, the accuracy, fairness or independence of your journalism. Do not improperly use a journalistic position for personal gain.

6. Do not allow advertising or other commercial considerations to undermine accuracy, fairness or independence.

7. Do your utmost to ensure disclosure of any direct or indirect payment made for interviews, pictures, information or stories.

8. Use fair, responsible and honest means to obtain material. Identify yourself and your employer before obtaining any interview for publication or broadcast. Never exploit a person's vulnerability or ignorance of media practice.

9. Present pictures and sound which are true and accurate. Any manipulation likely to mislead should be disclosed.

10. Do not plagiarise.

11. Respect private grief and personal privacy. Journalists have the right to resist compulsion to intrude.

12. Do your utmost to achieve fair correction of errors.

Guidance Clause: Basic values often need interpretation and sometimes come into conflict. Ethical journalism requires conscientious decision-making in context. Only substantial advancement of the public interest or risk of substantial harm to people allows any standard to be overridden.

CHAPTER 17

On the record, on background and off the record

- Understand the differences between on the record, on background and attribution to

- Never say anything you don't want reported

- Take care with attribution – you may be identified

- Be careful about going on and off the record during an interview

Even experienced media collaborators and journalists do not agree on the precise meaning of these terms.

To be safe, it's wise to ensure that you and a reporter are clear on the rules under which you are operating. There is also nothing legally binding about any of these terms so you should trust the journalist to honour any agreements reached.

On the record

One undisputed rule is that once a journalist has identified him or herself as a reporter for a media outlet, everything you say after that is on the record which means everything can be reported and attributed to you.

For novices particularly, the safest option is not to say anything in front of a journalist or within range of a microphone that you do not want reported. This includes when you are having a relaxed drink in a pub or lolling back with your feet on the desk just shooting the breeze with a reporter.

If you do have a very good reason for providing information that cannot be seen as coming from you, then make sure you know what you are doing.

On background and not for attribution

These are messy.

To some, they mean the information can be reported but its source must be kept confidential. The information may be paraphrased or given as a direct quote from an unidentified source. However, this can become tricky when someone who is described as 'a source close to the negotiation' turns out to be one of two or three people in a room whose identity is easily discoverable. If you are going to be described by something other than your name, it's best to agree on the precise attribution with the journalist to prevent being identified.

On background can also be taken to mean that the information is for background only and cannot be reported in any way: it's just to give a journalist some context or a new perspective.

Off the record

This means the information cannot be reported at all and the source cannot be revealed. This does not stop a journalist using that information if they also get it later from another source who is *on the record*.

Confused? It gets worse.

Switching on and off

In the middle of an interview some people will say: 'This is *off the record*' and then keep talking. The problem for the journalist – who may not want to interrupt a flow of useful information – is what happens when the interviewee doesn't say: 'We are now back *on the record*'.

Which bits of the interview are in? Which bits are out? Was it just one piece of information that was *off the record* or was all the rest of the interview not for public disclosure? Going on and off the record frequently in an interview can be incredibly frustrating and a bit dangerous if you and the journalist are not on the same page.

For novices particularly, the safest option is not to say anything in front of a journalist or within range of a microphone that you do not want reported.

CHAPTER 18

Dealing with tricky situations

- Say no to an interview if it's not your area of expertise or you don't have time

- Consider passing the interview to a colleague

- Decline if you think there's an agenda or you're being set up

- Was it a mistake or malicious?

- How to take action on inaccuracies

Why and how academics say no to journalists

There would be few journalists who have not had to find a way to politely decline the offer of a story from someone who is particularly passionate about their story's news value. It can be a tricky situation, particularly when the storyteller won't back off and the journalist is in a social setting with no route for escape.

Likewise, academics can feel pressured by journalists to be involved in stories they would rather avoid. Below are the reasons academics have given for knocking back journalists' requests. The quotes are unattributed to protect academic-journalist relationships.

They do not have the answer

Very early on in my career, I said 'yes' and answered something where I didn't have enough information. The next day I got some severely reprimanding emails from senior academics pointing out that I didn't know what I was talking about on that topic. So that put me in my place and I learnt a lesson from that.

We all feel compelled to try and give an answer, even if we're not totally sure. You've got to learn to deal with that with practise and maturity.

Don't just say something because you want to hear the sound of your own voice or see your name in print. Do it because you have something genuine to say.

The request falls too far outside their area of expertise

I always ask for examples of the questions that they might ask. I'm usually just really trying to understand if I am really going to be able to add value in a way that helps tell the narrative or get to the insight needed.

I tend to say, 'I don't feel like I can talk on that topic to the extent that maybe you need'.

I never say an outright 'no'. I always say it would be better if you talk to this person and then help them do their job.

I try to be positive by passing them on to somebody who might be more knowledgeable than I am on that particular area.

I will be asked to comment on all sorts of things that I often don't know the answer to. So I field it to other people in my department, in the university or the business school.

They do not have time to prepare and do not feel well-versed on the topic

If A rings me and says: 'Do you have five minutes?' I'll say: 'I can't talk to you right now but I can call you back between three and four, or what time are you available this afternoon?' Then I'll get my thoughts together and think about the messages. And it gives me a chance to ask them: 'What's the angle of this story? Am I the right person?'

They really do not have time to talk

If you don't have the time, say 'no'. A little bit of scarcity with journalists can also be quite valuable, so you don't have to respond to every request.

I say:'Look, I'm sorry. I'm teaching or I'm giving seminars all day or I'm super busy with something else and would normally like to help, but sorry, I'm just too busy today.'

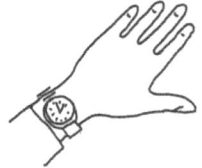

It's a cold call from a journalist working for a media platform of limited value to the academic

It does take time to do these things and, if it hasn't got the reach in the readership, then I'm probably not going to do it.

They do not think the journalist is trustworthy or works for a credible organisation

Most journalists are respectful of the help you give them and the role you're playing in helping them communicate with the broader community through their work. But yeah, there are more what you might call tabloid-y type institutions, whether it be a TV channel or a newspaper or I'm sure there's plenty of them out there in digital land.

Sometimes it's just unintelligent, boring commentary. In one case I recognised his name and I had a similar distrust of the publications that he worked in. So I just didn't return his call. So you have to be kind of beware.

They think the journalist may be setting them up or there's an underlying agenda

I don't ever want to be in a 'gotcha' moment. I've been in a 'gotcha' moment once. I felt inexperienced and I should have stood up for myself.

If I am really worried about the hook or the agenda of the story I usually won't say 'no' because I think it's really important to communicate with people that wouldn't normally otherwise agree with us. And so I'd be just careful about what's my messaging, what's my responses when I get asked the really challenging questions, and prep for what's the worst possible thing they could ask me. And then occasionally, if I think I'm really going to be set up, I might say 'no'.

There's a potential conflict of interest

If I was being approached (which has happened a few times by a PR company on behalf of an organisation who's wanting to put some messaging out relating to a product) and they want you to provide expert comment that's going into some sort of advertorial relating to that product, I would always say 'no' because I think it's a huge conflict of interest.

They may not be able to deal with the potential fallout

Some topics tend to generate more vitriol from the public than others. If you're talking about things that are politically oriented, which is often the case in the press, there can be a public backlash against what you say. Sometimes they're going to say some nasty, horrible, mean things about you and you have to be emotionally prepared for that. You need a kind of thick skin to be able to take that.

When they are just one of many

I almost say 'no' to every story when I know that they will call multiple people; where you have the sort of articles where four people get one quote – nobody knows you, nobody cares. So I will only do stories with journalists where I am the only expert and it's really a request for my view on things and not just to have any academic.

They are asked to comment on behalf of the university when they are comfortable talking solely as an individual about their area of expertise

You've got to know the boundary yourself. There are just lines you've got to draw.

Correcting journalists

Avoiding inaccurate or wildly out-of-context reportage should start with steering well clear of any dodgy journalists.

'I don't think there are many journalists who fall in that camp, but it's worth doing the research and finding out who they are. If somebody's really got a reputation for verballing people, don't deal with them. Don't talk to them,' John Ross, Asia-Pacific Editor of *Times Higher Education*, says.

If the journalist is credible then it's up to you to deliver clear messages that lessen the chance of ambiguity or inaccuracy. However, it can also be smart to double-check that your messages have been received accurately.

Be polite but direct

ABC Education Reporter Conor Duffy advises treating an interview like a conversation in which you might gently correct an error during the conversation.

'Be polite, but also direct. If someone's asking you questions, and you're getting a sense that they don't really understand what they're talking about, then I would be worried about how they were going to represent what I said. I think an academic in that situation should be pretty direct and not feel that they have to give an answer that a journalist wants them to give.

'Most journalists work in pretty robust environments in newsrooms. Things are pretty quick and feedback's often very blunt. We're pretty thick skinned or you don't survive long,' Duffy says.

Misunderstanding, muck up or malicious?

How you proceed will affect your media relationship so you need to weigh up what is at stake: is it just a minor error in a fleeting story, or part of an investigative story gone wrong which can have wider and deeper repercussions? (If the latter, it would be worth seeking legal advice before acting.)

Most stuff ups will be due to a misunderstanding rather than malicious intent and should initially be treated that way.

Journalist John Ross suggests taking a little time to cool off if you are really upset with a story. 'Try and start from a point that, if the journalist has done something that you think is really wrong, the journalist has probably done so inadvertently. That won't always be the case, but I think it probably often is.

'The journalist might have a different way of looking at whatever information was available and interpreted it in a certain way, which may even be a reasonable way to interpret it or could be just an honest misinterpretation,' Ross says.

Harangued because of headlines

The *Australian Financial Review's* Julie Hare says headlines on stories have caused her the most grief over her many years of reporting.

Those headlines are not usually written or controlled by the journalist; they are the domain of sub-editors. So being blamed can be particularly galling for the journalist in the firing line.

It doesn't excuse the publication of an unfair headline but at least it becomes clear who is at fault.

Checks and balances

Conor Duffy says the level of checking varies wildly between media outlets. There are those with lots of checks before stories are broadcast or published right through to outlets that may take a punt that a story is good enough to be worth any legal action that follows.

'But I think it's always best to resolve things amicably if you can. Most places, especially now with digital journalism being at the forefront of everything, are pretty open to making corrections or clarifications,' Duffy says.

Taking action

All journalists interviewed agree that the first point of call should be a respectful conversation with the journalist about the story, so you can ascertain what happened. This is infinitely better than unnecessarily embarrassing the journalist in front of bosses or peers or unfairly berating him or her.

Julie Hare says: 'Contact the journalist and say: *You misquoted me. I didn't say that. That's out of context.* And try and get it changed online. Most journalists are open to changing something if they misunderstood something or just got something slightly out of context. I think the hope is that you just don't have to do it too often.'

If you are not happy with the journalist's response, you may decide to escalate the complaint to the person in charge, normally the editor or executive producer.

The authorities of last resort (besides the courts) are the Australian Press Council or Australian Communications and Media Authority (ACMA) but be prepared to wait quite a while for a result.

4

Building and boosting your public profile

CHAPTER 19

Working with communications teams

- Why utilise your university communications team?

- How to find the right journalists for your subject areas

- Keep your LinkedIn profile and other social media up to date

- *The Conversation*: a good way to have media find you

- Why building mutual trust with media is important

- How other academics started boosting their public profiles

You have something to say, you've distilled the points of most interest to your audience and you can deliver that knowledge in an engaging way. But now what?

You could start by reaching out to media on your own – which can be successful – or you could seek the advice of communications experts in your institution.

Some schools or faculties have dedicated communications staff, but comms teams are being increasingly centralised in universities. If the latter, find out if one particular team member focuses on your area of expertise and give them a call.

" *They're just a really valuable resource for you to brainstorm ideas and say: 'I think this is a story, but I'm not sure, can I throw around a few ideas?'* **"**

CATHERINE WEBBER, *BOND UNIVERSITY*

You should let your communications team know about your noteworthy work so they can judge whether you have a story likely to interest traditional media, trade or industry outlets, higher education publications and/or social media platforms.

" *You need to have a journalist's ability to see what people will read.* **"**

STEPHEN MATCHETT, *CAMPUS MORNING MAIL*

Many communications team are composed of journalists who know what constitutes a news story; what may work better as part of a larger feature piece; who writes, creates and publishes what type of content; and the best ways to package an offering to make it attractive to targeted audiences.

Tim Dodd, Higher Education Editor of *The Australian*, says: 'It's really important to have a good comms team, people who can really sift out what is happening in that university, which has a good media angle, which will make a story.'

The team should also have relationships with trusted journalists and be on top of current issues.

Teams link journalists to experts

Journalists will often ask university communications teams to source relevant experts to add to their stories.

Therefore, it is worth ensuring your communications team knows what you are up to, your specific interests and areas of expertise.

" Communications teams will express frustration to me about the willingness of academics to make themselves available for media interviews – particularly on the television side – that obviously involve a lot more time. "

CONOR DUFFY, *AUSTRALIAN BROADCASTING CORPORATION*

Some communications teams frequently send the media lists of experts who will be available for comment on upcoming newsworthy events. If your organisation doesn't do that, you could send a text or email to relevant journalists to let them know that you are available for timely analysis and/or commentary on the release of a report relevant to your area of expertise.

Finding a journalist

It's often quite easy to find a journalist's email, social media handles and even phone numbers through a quick search online. If that fails, you can telephone the organisation and ask for the person's email.

However, if you want to help people find you, don't rely solely on your organisational affiliations. Maintain an up-to-date personal LinkedIn profile and ensure that it, and any other social media platforms you use, include descriptors that outline your field of expertise, your organisation and any additional contact details you are comfortable making public.

Bond University's Catherine Webber points out the ease of connecting on Twitter. 'Journalists are so available that their emails are on their Twitter handles. Or just drop them a line, follow them on Twitter and try and get into that,' she suggests.

On the other side of the fence, *The Australian Financial Review's* Julie Hare finds *The Conversation*[38] useful in identifying academics who are open to communicating outwardly. (You must be connected to a higher education institution to write for *The Conversation*, which helps academics publish evidence-backed articles in accessible language on a free online platform.)

The good, the bad and the in between

Journalists say there are good and bad communications teams, which may get better or worse depending on who is in charge.

The good ones respond to requests as quickly and effectively as possible and provide useful background.

'They're very across the issues that are in the public space being debated. And when you go to them, they've already sort of anticipated that. For example, with university research funding, some of the schools have been very good at doing their own work, talking to researchers and seeing who would be good to put up to make the sector's case,' ABC Education Reporter, Conor Duffy, says.

John Ross, Asia-Pacific editor of *Times Higher Education,* says communications teams are important as a middle layer between him and university administrators he needs to talk to. They are also usually really good for having a non-attributable, fairly honest, background conversation about things.

'Sometimes you might think you're on to a red-hot story but you've been sold a bit of a dud,' Ross says. 'University comms people usually have enough trust with journalists like me, anyway, to be able to express that. I might not necessarily take their word for it, but often I might do more investigations which I wouldn't have done if we hadn't had that conversation.

'We exist to inform the higher education sector, and we don't do that if we're peddling nonsense essentially. You don't want to be the bunny that's been sold a lemon,' Ross says.

Less helpful communications teams may come back with meaningless replies to questions or block access to spokespeople.

Conor Duffy finds a lot of university leaders are reluctant to give on-camera interviews.

'As a sector, that's a bit of a missed opportunity because obviously these people are leaders for a reason. And sometimes, from a media perspective, it feels like there's a very expensive PR apparatus around them designed to stop me from getting access to them.'

Some communications staff try to 'heavy' journalists over stories they do not like, but the worst teams are like black holes where media requests go to die.

'They don't get back to you, they just don't seem to be bothered. Or you get someone really junior who just doesn't really get it. The dreadful ones don't engage. And that goes for the lobby groups too,' Julie Hare of *The Australian Financial Review* says.

Hare appreciates developing long-standing relationships with mutual trust and not having to 'ring that awful bloody landline or use that [general] media email and not get anything...I can't stand that generic stuff. People don't put their names and phone numbers on things. I hate it.'

ABC Senior Business Correspondent, Peter Ryan, bemoans being spammed by emails that go to everyone and/or receiving phone calls from an inexperienced person, even an intern, when it would be more helpful to be contacted directly by someone with a lot more knowledge and gravitas.

He also says frequent turnover of staff in communications teams can make it difficult to build relationships – a criticism that those working with journalists make in return, as journalists are often on the move. This emphasises the importance of keeping media lists up to date.

38 See https://www.theconversation.com.au

CHAPTER 20

Making the most of media training

- Don't wing it – use media training if you can

- Hone your presentation and practise out loud

- Learn the art of short sound bites – media will love you

- Dealing with tricky, unexpected questions

- How to grab attention with 'hooks' in your media material

Media training can help you understand how the media operate and what they want. At its core is hands-on training in how to distil and convey key messages – something of benefit well beyond media interviews. So, if your university offers that training, embrace the opportunity and consider doing it more than once to update your media skills.

Nicole Hartley of UQ Business School says even her expertise in marketing and advertising does not cover structuring comms that are clear, concise, relevant and add value to your target audience. 'It's not something we are trained in unless we do the media training that's provided,' she says.

> **"** *If you're going to drone on, no one is going to be interested. The university media officers really can play a very large role here in helping.* **"**
>
> **STEPHEN MATCHETT,** *CAMPUS MORNING MAIL*

Even experienced media performers can benefit from honing the presentation of a specific piece of work or new knowledge they are conveying.

> **"** *It is very helpful to have some good advice and mentoring about how to approach it. I still have coaching in media and a PR support who helps me get stories in the media.* **"**
>
> **ELIZABETH SHEEDY,** *MACQUARIE BUSINESS SCHOOL*

The ones who make interviews look relaxed and easy have usually spent a great deal of time over the years preparing what they want to say before talking publicly.

Never be too cocky to accept constructive criticism because anyone can be tripped up or dig themselves into a hole during an interview.

You need to know your stuff, have practised answering questions related to your issue OUT LOUD in front of someone (they always sound better just in your head) and be prepared to deal with any more general questions that may be tossed in – whether or not you feel comfortable answering them.

Ignoring questions or saying *no comment* won't win you any accolades.

There are ways to deal well with tricky moments so best to learn them, be clear about what you will and won't say, and know your personal boundaries early on.

Media training can also help you understand and be ready for whom you are talking to in the media.

> **"** *Particularly if you're starting out, you might find that you get someone who's abrasive or really confrontational and can throw you. So if you're a bit prepared for that, that can be helpful.* **"**
>
> **MARIAN BAIRD,** *THE UNIVERSITY OF SYDNEY BUSINESS SCHOOL*

For those more used to writing a dissertation, learning to do TV news sound bites (interview grabs) of eight to 12 seconds in length may seem of little value. However, journalist Conor Duffy says you need to weigh that up against the fact that an academic journal may reach a few thousand people whereas TV news may put you in front of a million – and that doesn't include those who watch the story later online.

When he started, QUT Business School's Gary Mortimer says he really struggled with doing those short interview bites, but media training exercises helped build his confidence and he has learned to build those grabs as hooks into written articles.

'So straight up you're saying: Here's something that's really, really interesting. And over the next 700 words, I'm going to tell you about it. Whereas my early work was: *Let's start with the introduction, let's do a bit of a lit review and let's do some findings at the bottom,* which was basically an article. So the writing is very different,' Professor Mortimer says.

He also found watching TED talks helped him work out what industry was interested in and the difference between 'standing in front of 300 first-year students and standing in front of a board or 200 retail leaders'.

But what if you don't have time for media engagement?

UTS Business School Dean, Carl Rhodes, says the work done in business schools – covering business, the economy and management – affects everybody in the world. Therefore, it's worth prioritising external communications.

He says academics have much more discretionary time than people in any other professions. 'So it's a question of how that discretion is used. If people say they don't have enough time, there's probably another reason they're really not doing it and it's not about the time.'

CHAPTER 21

Giving good interviews

- Prepare, prepare and prepare some more

- Who's the audience: think how to tailor your language and content

- What are your three key messages?

- Keep abreast of current issues and have responses ready

- Set your boundaries: what will you say or not say?

An interview should be a robust conversation, not you being led by the nose through a series of questions, which may or may not lead you up the proverbial garden path.

Think about those times you have been determined to get a point across in a lively conversation – you tend to find a way to do it. With practice, you can do the same thing in interviews in a friendly and engaging manner. Of course, this does not mean taking the one liner of the day, as many politicians do, and repeating it ad nauseam while ignoring the questions being asked.

Preparation, preparation, preparation

A large part of giving effective interviews relies on preparation, which means the work starts well before you begin speaking to the journalist.

If you are seen as an expert, you no doubt know your subject inside out. On the upside, you can draw easily on the knowledge required to answer questions. On the downward slope, it can mean having so much information swishing around in your brain that you may not easily discern the key points of most interest to your audience.

❝ *If you have all this information in your head, then the best preparation you can do is try and get some of it out. If you've been consumed with something and it's your niche, you understand it so well that you start a conversation assuming everyone has the assumed knowledge that you have.* **❞**

CATHERINE WEBBER, *BOND UNIVERSITY*

Remember: a media interview is not just about talking to a journalist (no matter how famous they are). It is about reaching a specific audience through that journalist as the medium. Therefore you need to tailor your language and content to fit what the audience wants to learn.

Preparation involves having the necessary information at hand, distilling it down for the sake of clarity and knowing exactly what you want to convey.

'It's important to think *How can I get this across clearly, succinctly, use everyday language, not jargon?* Preparation is really important,' Libby Sander of Bond University, says.

Marian Baird of The University of Sydney Business School sees preparation as essential when you are new to doing interviews. But the more interviews you do, the more you see the same issues coming back and they require less preparation. However, Professor Baird always prepares for new topics.

The rule of three

As a rule of thumb, if you manage to get three clear messages out in one news interview you are doing very well. It is possible to give three clear points in 10 to 15 seconds but it takes practice to develop that skill.

Audiences of broadcast media are often multi-tasking and not giving their full attention, so when words fly past at three words per second, you need to be crystal clear to cut through. Not sure about that? The day after you've appeared on the news, ask someone who saw or heard your moment in the spotlight what you said. Their response is often very disappointing.

Readers can, of course, go back and re-read an article but it's going to have to very compelling for them to do that in this world of information overload.

Limbering up in advance

Many find it professionally useful to stay abreast of current issues in industry and more general media.

Like many journalists, Gary Mortimer of QUT Business School has a morning routine that begins with reading three newspapers to ensure he stays on top of business issues. As a retail expert, he is often asked to comment; most news organisations see retail consumers as their audience.

Professor Mortimer also prepares for events he knows are likely to arise. For example, the federal Pharmacy Agreement comes up for renewal every five years so he is likely to be part of the ongoing debate over whether we should put pharmacies in supermarkets.

Likewise, UNSW's Nick Wailes will prepare for issues. He drafts op-eds or other short pieces that provide him with working templates that help reduce the large amount of time often required when an issue snowballs in the media. He will also look out for interesting stories for which he may be able to offer journalists real-world examples.

When caught on the hop with a media request, Professor Wailes never takes it straight away. Instead, he will say he's happy to talk in a couple of hours and then spend that time getting up to speed on statistics, the data and any other relevant details. For reference, he jots down the key points to ensure everything he says in the interview is as accurate as possible.

Ask your own questions

Where possible, it's advisable to find out ahead of time the line being taken and the tone or possible agenda of the journalist and/or media outlet doing the story.

'I think some journalists would be offended if you asked them to give you all their questions and probably wouldn't, but I think all journalists would give you a sense of the line of questioning,' the ABC's Conor Duffy says.

But remember stories are usually works in progress.

'You can go into a story thinking it's going one way and then the story can flip and you realise it's going somewhere else. So, it's a very movable feast, journalism,' *The Australian Financial Review's* Julie Hare says.

Asking who else is being interviewed for the story can give you insights into the other points of view likely to be canvassed, but there may be levels of sensitivity or timing that may inhibit what a journalist can tell you.

'There's often times I genuinely don't know who else is in the story, or if someone is sort of teetering on the edge of committing to being in the story. But I think, yeah, you always ask. And you're absolutely justified in asking. But I wouldn't necessarily think that if someone can't tell you that it's for nefarious reasons,' Conor Duffy says.

Boundaries and preparing for any questions

Before an interview you should define (in your mind at least) the boundaries around what you can and cannot say.

Apart from not discussing subjects outside your area of expertise, it is important to distinguish between you as an expert individual academic as opposed to an official spokesperson for your institution. Usually, only specific people are approved to talk on behalf of your institution, so it is best not to spontaneously assume that mantle during an interview.

Journalists wouldn't be doing their job if they ignored opportunities to ask questions about hot issues, even if that is not the prime reason for the interview or you are not the designated organisational spokesperson.

Journalist Peter Ryan says, as much as they may not like it, even those handling corporate public relations 'realise that once they get the boss in the room in front of a microphone, it's all up to the boss. That's why they're on the big bucks – they've got to answer the questions'.

Ryan adds that most people are able to handle additional questions in some form but, he says, 'any chief executive or anyone who goes into an interview should be prepared to have other things sprung on them, within reason'.

This is where it can be helpful to discuss potential touchy or tricky subjects with your university communications person or colleague with extensive media experience, and practise how you will respond. Better to prepare for disarming, out-of-field questions and hope for the best.

Interview check list

Prepare the content

- Be very clear on why you are doing the interview and the content of your key messages

- Distil the essence of your messages so that you do not bury your two or three key messages under too much information, a deluge of statistics and/or endless acronyms and jargon

- Break complex figures or messages down to the simplest form before the interview

- Look for good analogies that may help to explain a complicated point

- Ensure you understand the specific focus and audience of the interviewer

- Think about the questions you are likely to encounter and practise your answers. Even a colleague running a few questions past you over the telephone is better than no preparation at all

- Your answers may sound perfectly composed in your mind, but they will sound different when you road test them out loud. It's always best to warm up before an interview.

Be conversational but get your messages out

- Convey your key messages in a knowledgeable, friendly and enthusiastic manner

- Talk through the journalist to your audience in language they will understand

- Remember you have the rights of normal conversation in an interview. Just because an interviewer may ask something inappropriate does not mean you have to answer in the way the interviewer wants

- If an interviewer uses inflammatory words in a question, be careful not to repeat those words in your answer unless you like the phrase. It will be your answer, not their question, that will stand alone as the quotable quote

- Do not allow journalists to catch you on the hop. Gather your thoughts before answering questions. However, if you say you will call the journalist back in 10 minutes, do call back at the specified time. A couple of minutes may not matter to you, but it can mean the difference between making a news bulletin or missing out.

Stay on the record

- Assume EVERYTHING is on the record unless you are a very experienced media performer and you trust the journalist

- If there is electronic equipment nearby assume you can be recorded. Microphones can pick up things you can't hear.

Choose a good location

- Think about the location you offer for an interview. Does it visually or aurally reinforce your message? Is it too noisy? Windy? Is there an air conditioner or loud refrigerator that will interfere with the recording of sound?
- Is there enough room for a camera operator to stand back from where you are sitting? Are there any other distractions or forms of interference?

Look good

- For video interviews, always check how you look. It is not about being vain. An upturned collar or unruly bit of hair can distract a viewer who will then miss what you say in the interview
- Are you appropriately dressed for the story? Feel comfortable in what you are wearing
- Avoid fine stripes that strobe, jangling jewellery or anything else that can distract you, the interviewer or the viewer
- Just before the interview starts, always ask the cameraperson if everything looks straight. That gives the cameraperson permission to tell you if it's not.

A DOZEN DIFFERENT WAYS OF BOOSTING PUBLIC PROFILES

Dr Freya Higgins-Desbiolles, Senior Lecturer in Tourism Management, UniSA Business.

A tourism article on noble savage imagery which coincided with an Indigenous conference kick started the building of Dr Freya Higgins-Desbiolles' profile. The article was picked up by ABC Radio, both because of its evocative language and its conference timing.

'It was just the right moment at the right time,' Dr Higgins-Desbiolles says. 'But it was *The Conversation* that generated the profile I have now.'

Observing what other academics were writing about, she began pitching ideas which generated media interest and 'it just snowballed'.

Dr Higgins-Desbiolles also benefited from advice given by Michele Nardelli of the university's media department.

'The one thing she said that I'll never forget is: *Always deliver to the journalist. And if you can't give them what they want, then you tell them how they can get what they want. And if you can't do that, then you send them to me, and I'll get what they want.*'

Dr Higgins-Desbiolles continues to follow this

advice. When a TV opportunity arose on a topic for which she was not well suited, she passed it to a colleague with whom she did not have a strong relationship. The colleague did an excellent job, and their relationship improved.

'If you're not the right person, you shouldn't take it. My media guys didn't say to me that I should have taken it. In that one, his expertise was perfect. He did it really well. So that's something you ask: *How do we foster this in people?*

'We need to help people build that – and some people aren't going to be very good at it. I had a military supervisor for my master's thesis, and he told me the army actually made all of their guys do presentations and record them. Then you look at it yourself and you get professional feedback from people higher up than you.'

Dr Libby Sander, Assistant Professor of Organisational Behaviour, Bond University

While Libby Sander has not consciously gone about building a profile, she has always been aware that when she gets right into the depth of her research it tends to become quite narrow and very niche.

'I think that's true for any academic if we're going to get published in top journals,' Dr Sander says.

Dr Sander discusses with her students how they can extrapolate up to a broader topic that is of interest to a specific business audience or the general public.

Her research involves a lot about cognition, emotion and relational outcomes of the physical work environment, both in organisations and at urban levels.

'If we generalise that, I tend to do a lot on the future of work. And that also comes from my background, because I was a human resources director and an organisational consultant for a long time before I became an academic.

'So I take that broader lens about work and the workplace.'

Professor Carl Rhodes, Professor of Organisation Studies and Dean, UTS Business School

Carl Rhodes first started regular media involvement about five or six years ago after observing the activities of other academics.

'It seemed to me that it was a valuable thing to do. And I thought I had some views that people might like reading,' Professor Rhodes says.

While more interested in writing for the media than giving comments, Professor Rhodes does both.

'It's just become a part of my work,' he says.

Professor Elizabeth Sheedy, Risk Governance, Macquarie Business School

Risk governance in financial institutions became a hot topic in the media a few years back, and the interest has not abated.

So when Elizabeth Sheedy, a risk governance expert, found media beating a path to her office, she found it 'a little nerve wracking because the issues are so controversial'.

'But I decided I was going to face the challenge,' says Professor Sheedy, who had research findings that were relevant to the industry. She has now had media involvement for some seven years.

Dr Michael Callaghan, Lecturer in Marketing and Management, Deakin University

Michael Callaghan never made a conscious decision to build his public profile but had been involved in a broad range of activities from marketing through ethics and corporate governance to human resources and management.

'Because I have a very broad span of knowledge over a long period of time, I never felt the need to try and narrow that down to one area to brand myself as being a particular person,' says Dr Callaghan.

'There are researchers out there who feel if you do spread yourself so thin, you lose relevance in terms of what your area of research is. And maybe I'm a little bit guilty of that.

'But I do feel that part of the branding of me is somebody who has a lot of experience across a large amount of information. That actually enables me to make critical commentary about marketing things that involve ethics, and about ethics-related things that might involve strategic management.'

Dr Callaghan has cultivated a lot of relationships with journalists, including a couple with whom he catches up every week, even though this may not result in stories.

Talking with journalists on a regular basis feeds into his very broad range of understanding and engagement with the world, which he feels makes him a better, more relevant teacher.

Adjunct Professor Warren Hogan, Economist, UTS Business School

Warren Hogan has been speaking to the media since his younger days, and says you build your profile by being available and being constructive.

'It's a two-way thing,' says Adjunct Professor Hogan.

'They want someone to quote, they want an expert. But there's more to it than that. There's the relationship. So, you as an expert can be very useful to a journalist by being available to have a chat, to talk not about the story that day, but to help them build their expertise.

'I actually say it's a public service to help the journalists be better.'

Professor Debbie Haski-Leventhal, Professor in Management, Macquarie Business School

Debbie Haski-Leventhal's goal was to do well in her academic life and be promoted. She joined university in a junior capacity and worked hard for promotion.

'But I'm always driven by the desire to create a positive, meaningful impact. So it was always in my mind, *what can I do to promote this work and engage more people in it?*' says Professor Haski-Leventhal.

Professor Rae Cooper, Gender, Work and Employment Relations, The University of Sydney Business School

Rae Cooper was 'absolutely forced' to do her first media interview as nobody else was available. She was also made to do media training and hated the first three months of media interviews.

'Then I just realised it's kind of like lecturing. So first semester is hell, you over-prepare and you are probably the best you ever are in terms of your performance in front of a class. Then you get how to do this.

'It's the same kind of thing. I woke up one day and went, *oh, I'm doing media,'* says Professor Cooper.

'I quite like it – but it depends – there are some outlets I have spoken to who I will never speak to again.'

Professor Raymond Da Silva, Professor of Finance, UWA

Raymond Da Silva enjoys publicity work 'to a degree', and found he got a lot more positive feedback after he wrote a textbook some years ago.

'People said: *Oh, you wrote a textbook,'* says Da Silva, Professor of Finance at UWA, who also appears in cases requiring an expert witness.

While many academics may regard a book contract as a lesser achievement than getting a journal article in a top publication, Da Silva notes that many more people will read a textbook than an academic article.

Professor Julia Richardson, School of Management and Marketing, Curtin University

Julia Richardson had something of a 'mid-life crisis' when she questioned whether all her articles in academic journals really mattered.

'I remember I slogged and slogged over this article to get it published. I think it took me two years of my life that I'll never get back,' Professor Richardson says.

'Then I looked at some stats on it and I realised that something like 180 people had read it.'

Professor Richardson realised that her public talks on her area of research generated the most feedback and decided that was where she could have the most impact.

'So it was at that point that I thought I've got to get more of those *Conversation* pieces.'

Dr Louise Grimmer, Senior Lecturer, Marketing, UTAS Business School

Louise Grimmer's first foray into media was an opinion piece for her local newspaper in Hobart.

'That started to get me thinking, *you know, I can do this. I can write about the things that I'm researching and teaching,*' Dr Grimmer says.

Dr Grimmer then wrote her first article for *The Conversation* with Gary Mortimer, Professor of Marketing and Consumer Behaviour at QUT. She believes the frequent publication of their articles shows they are of interest to the general public.

Professor Peter van Onselen, Politics and Policy, Griffith University and UWA

Peter Van Onselen's career straddles academia and media as a political commentator and author.

While working on his PhD, Professor van Onselen used his research as the basis for a handful of opinion pieces on political party databases and the invasion of privacy, and what that meant for the accumulation of data.

'It lent itself to a few op-eds because it was the idea of Big Brother is watching and should we be worried about this,' he says.

When he joined Edith Cowan University, he took over the office and phone number of an academic who did a lot of local media in WA. The media phone calls continued, and Professor van Onselen was happy to provide commentary.

'I don't know if this is a good thing for an academic to highlight, but I think my turn of phrase at the time was sufficiently tabloid for some of the journalists to go: This is great!'

'When I took the job at Edith Cowan Uni, I quite liked the idea of doing opinion pieces as well as doing my scholarly work. I knew I had to do the scholarly work to gain promotion. I knew I had to do the teaching because I wanted to. I enjoyed that side of it. That was probably what most attracted me to academia in the first place. But I had in the back of my mind the idea that I liked the idea of engaging publicly in particular areas,' Professor van Onselen says.

He later collaborated with fellow West Australian political scientist Wayne Errington, on op-eds and several political books and biographies.

'It helped me cut to the chase, stylistically,' says Professor van Onselen who recognised Errington was the better writer and that he could learn from him.

'I've become a better writer and a faster writer. So it is something that became natural to me. But the biggest thing I get out of it is to try and give a view on something for a wider audience, knowing that more people are going to read it, not just (and I don't mean 'just' in a pejorative sense), academic colleagues. It's getting read by a wider audience and hopefully it's giving them pause for thought.'

For video interviews, always check how you look. It is not about being vain. An upturned collar or unruly bit of hair can distract a viewer who will then miss what you say in the interview.

5

Giving your story legs

CHAPTER 22

Developing communication and content strategies

- How to develop a communication strategy and content strategy

- What do you want to achieve, what are your key messages, who is your audience?

- How and when will you distribute your messages?

- What content or assets do you already have?

- What assets can you develop: still and moving images, tweets, blogs and social media tiles?

To strategically convey your messages and develop a work plan, it's useful to devise both a communication and a content strategy.

Communication strategy

A communication strategy is effectively the why, when and where. It usually includes a high-level view of:

- What you want to achieve
- Your key messages
- Your target audiences and their needs and interests
- Ways to distribute your messages
- Potential timing of communication releases
- Potential risks and risk management strategies.

" A systematic approach to choosing platforms, setting goals, understanding your audience and actively listening will help ensure you are laying sufficient groundwork.[39] "

COMMUNICATING YOUR RESEARCH WITH SOCIAL MEDIA

Content strategy

A content strategy is the how and what side of things. This looks at ways to frame your messages to fit the communications strategy and develop content or 'assets'.

Assets can take many forms including text, still and moving images, podcasts, infographics and other data visualisations, tweets, blogs and social media tiles.

" *[Content is] really central to the whole thing. Content is made up of your thoughts, ideas, reflections and insights.* **"**

COMMUNICATING YOUR RESEARCH WITH SOCIAL MEDIA[40]

39 Mollett, A, Brumley, C, Gilson. C & Williams. S. 2017. *Communicating Your Research with Social Media: A Practical Guide to Using Blogs, Podcasts, Data Visualisations and Video*, Sage Publishing, London
40 Ibid

To strategically convey your messages and develop a work plan, it's useful to devise both a communication and a content strategy.

CHAPTER 23

Knowing your audience

- Who are your audiences – there may be a number?

- How to identify your stakeholders and your detractors

- Group your stakeholders by common interests, establish their needs and how to best reach them

- How do they process information?

- How can you change their thinking and behaviour?

Knowing your audiences is the foundation for your communications and content strategy, so the earlier you start thinking about them the better.

Understanding to whom you are talking or would like to reach will influence your levels of information, style, language, format, tone and the methods of distribution most likely to hit the mark.

❝ The message must be one that is valuable to an audience based on their needs, delivered by a messenger they can trust, in language they are comfortable with. ❞

A HANDBOOK ON KNOWLEDGE SHARING[42]

As early as possible in a project, it's valuable to brainstorm with colleagues (or even just yourself) to determine who will or may be interested in your work. There are many ways to do this: get them down on a whiteboard, mind-map, draw concentric circles outwards from those closest to you, use free stakeholder-mapping templates from the internet.

In the *Research Impact Handbook*,[43] Mark Reed says there is no such thing as a general public. The challenge is to establish which publics are likely to be most interested in your work, and which will benefit most from engaging with it.

He provides these prompts to identify stakeholders:

- Who will be affected by the research?
- Will the impacts be local, national or international?
- Who has the power to influence the outcomes of the research?
- Who are potential allies and opponents?
- What coalitions might build around the issues being researched?

- Are there people whose voices or interests in the issue may not be heard?
- Who will be responsible for managing the outcome?
- Who can facilitate or impede the outcome through their participation, non-participation or opposition?
- Who can contribute financial or technical resources towards the research?

Potential stakeholders may include representatives of local, state and federal governments, politicians and their advisors, those in higher education, media organisations and specific journalists, industry and trade representatives, advocacy groups, advisory bodies, community groups, not-for-profit organisations, other researchers and research organisations.

When you have identified the relevant stakeholders and grouped them into common clusters, it's time to drill down into each cluster's specific interests and chief means of sharing and receiving knowledge.

If you don't know the answers, find out. It may take only a few phone calls, or it could involve several sessions with potential target audiences to more fully analyse their communication needs and the best ways to reach them.

❝ There are a variety of different stakeholders in the scholarly community responsible for addressing academic dissemination in the digital age, including but not limited to academics, research funders, university administrators, librarians, publishers, taxpayers and the wider public, but, at the same time, each has their own set of requirements and preferences for how scholarly material might be made available. ❞

COMMUNICATING YOUR RESEARCH WITH SOCIAL MEDIA[44]

Questions to ask about your audiences

In *What More Can I Say? Why Communication Fails and What to Do About It,* author Dianna Booher[45] says questions reveal the kinds of information you need to know to change someone's thinking or behaviour.

Booher suggests asking:

- Where do they stand on an issue?
- What's important to them?
- What are their goals? Timelines? Limits?
- Who's important to them?
- Who influences them?
- How do they process information?
- What do their word choices tell you – are they primarily visual, verbal or conceptual in processing information?

Booher maintains that influencing a wide audience involves merging their streams of information into one river.

She says: 'You, as curator of part of their content, can open and close the floodgates at will to help merge the flow of new information into their streams. Consider whom you are trying to influence — specifically. Match their emotional mood. Open the gate at the appropriate time. Make it real and relevant for best results.'

42 Tsui, L. Chapman, SA, Schnirer, L & Stewart, S. 2006, *A Handbook on Knowledge Sharing: Strategies and Recommendations for Researchers, Policymakers, and Service Providers,* Community-University Partnership for the Study of Children, Youth, and Families, Alberta, Canada.
43 Reed, MS. 2018, *The Research Impact Handbook,* 2nd Edition, Fast Track Impact, London.
44 Mollett, A, Brumley, C, Gilson, C & Williams, S 2017, *Communicating Your Research with Social Media: A Practical Guide to Using Blogs, Podcasts, Data Visualisations and Video,* Sage Publishing, London
45 Booher, D. 2015. *What More Can I Say? Why Communication Fails and What to Do About It.* Prentice Hill Press.

CHAPTER 24

Tips for early career researchers and other newbies

- The benefits of developing new skills

- Collaborative writing can kick goals

- Young researchers succeed via Twitter

- Universities should promote more diverse voices

- Check out the organisations which precis research

Moving from being a media novice

Academic training teaches you to be a professional critic, ripping other people's ideas apart. However, academics may also be quite equivocal with their findings, saying something could happen but it would depend on a number of variables.

In contrast, Nick Wailes of UNSW explains that effective communication requires developing a new set of skills – a bit like PhD training.

'You need to say: *How am I going to develop the skills I need to be an effective communicator in a public forum*, be able to provide the insight that your background knowledge allows you to have and do it in a way that's digestible and relevant,' Professor Wailes says.

You may already know more than you realise if you understand the community around your field and the ways in which information is most effectively conveyed.

If you are deeply embedded in your research and the way your research interfaces with the issues you study in the world beyond universities, then you know already what the audience is interested in, because that's your passion. Follow the leads, follow what's there.

STEPHEN MATCHETT, *EDITOR, CAMPUS MORNING MAIL*

Publishing and PhDs

Over the past decade, QUT's Gary Mortimer has seen big changes in how PhD candidates and more experienced academics collaborate on writing for different purposes.

For example, he frequently writes with UTAS Business School's Louise Grimmer and collaborates with other graduates on grants.

'I'm really seeing that across QUT and the Business School today where professors and associate professors will work with lecturers and senior lecturers and HDR (higher degree research) students to get them publishing.'

He also says three-year plans are developed to break studies down into publishable pieces so, by the second year of a PhD, candidates already have a paper under review. 'Very strategically we are looking at how we mentor ECR's (early career researchers) through to getting jobs.'

"Anyone pursuing a PhD should be given specific training and encouragement to engage more broadly and to be able to demonstrate their knowledge and share their knowledge with the community and with different communities. "

JULIE RICHARDSON, *CURTIN BUSINESS SCHOOL*

Professor Richardson sees training as particularly important to boost the confidence of those who may be reticent to put themselves forward. She says a strategic imperative should be universities getting more diverse voices out there.

However, while she is very active in the media, Libby Sander of Bond University says it is important to recognise that some people are not going to be comfortable engaging with media.

'We need to acknowledge what our own preferences and strengths and weaknesses are. And there are many ways to engage with industry and engage with potential grant partners and to disseminate our research. So we shouldn't think this is the only way,' Dr Sander says.

A couple of media suggestions

Journalist Conor Duffy suggests that early career researchers can benefit from establishing a social media presence, probably on Twitter, where he has seen young researchers successfully put out some of their work.

Journalist John Ross looks at what's coming out of academic journals because the peer review process acts as a quality assurance mechanism. He advises getting on the radar of bodies that precis research, similar to the American Association for the Advancement of Science's Eureka Alert site.

CHAPTER 25

Doing a stocktake and developing content

- Your assets: what have you got, what do you need?

- Smart phones: use them to produce high-quality photos and recordings

- Do you need to budget for professional expertise?

- Check out the many uses of good video elements

- Remember: re-purpose and re-use

After working out what you want to say and how best to communicate with your target audiences, it's time to look closely at your assets.

The question here is: what have you already got and what more do you need?

You may already have pieces of writing, images and other content that can be re-purposed. But how can you build assets while also doing your scholarly work?

Recording your work in multiple ways

Your communications and content strategies should inform what you need in text, audio and visuals.

The ability to produce high-quality photos, audio recordings and videos on smart phones makes it easier than ever to develop assets. This also avoids the frustration of realising a story could have been boosted by great visuals if only someone had thought to capture those moments at the time. You can curate what you have down the track; the main thing is an early start in gathering and carefully filing relevant material as you go.

Depending on a team's abilities and workloads, some projects will require communications specialists and professional expertise in the production of graphics, photos, audio and video. These costs will need to be budgeted if expertise cannot be provided by your institution.

Research once, write often. Write often, distribute afar.

It pays to be thrifty with content. Aim to waste nothing, and re-use and re-purpose where you can.

For example, if you record a video, have a transcript done with times on it so you can easily locate the pieces of video you want. You can save a huge amount of pain doing an edit on paper before you start cutting the video. The script (which will be tweaked during the video edit) also gives you the transcript of the story to post with the video content.

You may want short bits of video for promotional purposes and social media, which can be made from the original video. If the quality is high enough you can pull still images from a video for use as pictures to accompany stories.

If you split the audio off the video, you have the basis of a podcast. It too can be scripted using the time-coded transcript as a guide.

The transcript will also be the foundation for written articles and pulling out quotable quotes.

All this reflects a freelance journalist's mentality of research once and write often. Or write once and sell it often.

It's all about getting maximum bang for your time and bucks.

DOING MORE WITH EXISTING RESEARCH

Marian Baird of The University of Sydney Business School says they often put data they have previously used into new scenarios that make it much more palatable for their audiences and the journalists.

'One strategy that was very successful was to say: *Look, we know from our research what it cost to raise a child, what the parental leave is, what the provisions are and how long women are taking off. Now, let's apply that to women in teaching in Adelaide, women in retail in Brisbane.*

'So you build scenarios from the material that you've already researched and put that as a report,' Professor Baird says.

It may not be an academic work, but Professor Baird says it's very effective, based on evidence and properly referenced using ABS statistics.

CHAPTER 26

Media releases

- Media releases: your lead may be in your research conclusions

- One page only, plus a page for background if necessary

- The eight key inclusions for every media release

- Active not passive language, keep it brief and clear, avoid jargon and cliches

- Double check content, road test, get someone else to proofread

Media releases are useful for conveying your messages. They are usually written like news stories with compelling headlines; an active, clear and concise style of writing; the most important elements at the start (these may often come from your research conclusions); and direct quotes from one or more people.

Media conferences are sometimes referred to as press conferences or pressers; likewise, media releases are sometimes called press releases. To be inclusive, it's best to stick with 'media' and not unwittingly annoy those in broadcasting or online.

The technical stuff

- **Keep the media release to one A4 page** but don't cheat by using a font smaller than 11-point or ridiculously narrow page margins. If there is too much information, you can provide background or relevant facts on a second page

- **A media release headline should be punchy and no more than one line long** (up to about six words). You could add a short subheading but only do so if that second point is vital

- **Date the media release** at the top of the page

- If it involves an event, **ensure the event date, time and location are also at the top**

- **Detail any spokespeople available** for interviews

- **Detail any audio, video and/or still images available** for media use

- **Put the name, title, email address and mobile phone number of one or two contacts at the bottom of the A4 page.** Ensure one contact is available from early morning to late at night to account for different time zones and news deadlines
- **Include social media handles** like @businessdeans for Twitter or your LinkedIn address.

The content

- **The most important points of the release should be at the top.** If you haven't grabbed the media's attention in the first paragraph or two, your release will probably hit the bin
- **Include direct quotes** from your spokesperson or spokespeople.

The writing style

- **Write in an active, not passive manner.** Active: The cat sat on the mat. Passive: The mat was sat on by the cat
- **Keep language simple and to the point.** You are aiming for brevity and clarity
- **Be specific. Say exactly what you mean.** Eg: What is a facility? A toilet block? The Melbourne Cricket Ground? An office? A search and rescue base?
- **Do not use many words when one will suffice.** Eg: *most* is better than *the majority of.* Do you need to a*sk a question* or simply *question*?
- **Do not put too many ideas into one sentence.** Never underestimate the value of a full stop

- **Do not put two sentences into one paragraph**. Short, sharp paragraphs are the style – like paragraphs in newspaper stories
- **Do not use unnecessary or meaningless modifiers**. Eg: anonymous stranger, advance warning or collaborate together
- **Avoid clichés.** They are overused, lazy and boring
- **Avoid jargon.** It gets in the way of communicating well with people outside your field of expertise. It's like talking shop to someone who has no idea what you mean
- **Avoid, or at least explain, acronyms.** If you must use acronyms, spell out the full name and put the acronym in brackets the first time it is used. Eg: Queensland University of Technology (QUT). You may then use the acronym in the rest of the media release.

Checks and balances

- **Double check the meaning of words and spelling**. Do not rely solely on spell check. Watch out for American spellings, particularly the use of a z instead of an s. For example, organization (US spelling) instead of organisation (Australian spelling)
- **Road test your media release** on a couple of people who know nothing about its subject matter. Do they understand it all? Is every point clear?
- **Make sure at least one other person proofreads** your media release and checks for typos and other glitches. Even small mistakes detract from your credibility so it's worth paying attention to detail.

CHAPTER 27

Opinion pieces

- Find those new insights in your field

- Write clearly, write for readability

- Your introduction must be really compelling

- Give a well-informed opinion

- Call others to action

The best opinion pieces provoke a response and challenge the reader to think in new ways.

Tim Dodd, Higher Education Editor for *The Australian*, says: 'We're looking for things which say something new, which give people insights that they might not have thought of, and which are well written and clearly written.'

The regular contributors have a history of saying new things in a readable way. 'Everyone has limited time and limited attention and we actually need to offer stories which people are going to think are worth their time,' Dodd says.

Dodd decides which pieces will be accepted for publication in the Higher Education section but, like most media outlets, there are Opinion Page or Comment Editors responsible for the general Opinion and Editorial (op-ed) pages.

In the global publication, *Times Higher Education*, the Opinion Editor is based in London but pieces from Australia and New Zealand should be submitted first to John Ross, the Asia-Pacific Editor.

Times Higher Education opinion pieces have to focus on higher education policy and 'be recognisable as something that's of relevance to a global audience, even if it doesn't immediately affect everybody in the global audience. But beyond that the field can be pretty broad,' Asia-Pacific Editor, John Ross says.

Writing opinion pieces

Opinion pieces are usually no more than 700 words long.

They need to open strongly with the main points, which often provide a new take on a current issue.

'You have to have an introduction so compelling that people are going to be forced to read to the end because they just can't do anything else,' Tim Dodd says.

The media outlet's audience needs to be able to relate to the language used and understand the level of authority, evidence and expertise supporting the arguments made.

There's no point in pussy footing about when writing an opinion piece. You need the ability – and sometimes a large dose of courage – to say exactly what you mean, even when there is likely to be push back from those opposed to your views.

Provide an informed opinion, not a rant

Opinion pieces can be a terrific way to maintain control over your content, unlike when you are interviewed and the journalist selects the elements for a story.

But in media outlets that aspire to providing balance, opinion pieces are not vehicles for ranting without supporting evidence. Best to leave that to columnists who trade on creating controversy (often fact-free), personal blogs and social media feuds.

Nor should you diminish your credibility by trying to camouflage promotion of a product behind a thin veneer of commentary.

Call others to action

You may be writing for the joy of seeing your name and face in print. However, we assume you are really more interested in writing an opinion piece because you want something to change.

Take the time to hone your main point or points so they hit the mark with stiletto-like precision.

Then write to persuade with passion, expertise and conviction.

*Opinion pieces can be a terrific way
to maintain control over your content,
unlike when you are interviewed and
the journalist selects the elements for
a story.*

CHAPTER 28

Blog, blogging away

- What's the difference between blogs and opinion pieces?

- Blogs can reach much wider audiences

- Consider four types of blogs – which is best for you?

- What about your content and frequency?

- Five good uses of blogs

Opinion pieces can always be used as blogs, but all blogs will not be suitable opinion pieces.

So what's the difference?

Once we could have argued that opinion pieces were the articles in close proximity to the editorial in a newspaper, while blogs were confined to the internet. But given the cutbacks in the size of newspapers, a lot of opinion pieces now only show up on media websites.

So perhaps the best explanation is that blogs are much less constrained than opinion pieces and tend not to be behind paywalls.

Blogs can range from photos and writing about cooking or gardening with Australian native daisies right through to extremely granular data analysis of interest to a very narrow but deep field of expertise. They are also excellent ways to document your reflections, ideas and research progress and build collegial networks.

❝ *Creating accessible blog posts about your research, studies or projects can be painless and quick, and is a great route to opening up your content to wider audiences.* **❞**

COMMUNICATING YOUR RESEARCH WITH SOCIAL MEDIA[46]

Academic blogging

The authors of *Communicating Your Research with Social Media*[47] highlight the 'growing opportunities for public-facing, digital research content' and 'the more informal, question-led content that appears across the academic blogosphere'.

Mollett et al. say the four types of blogs used by UK academics comprise:

- **University-based blog sites** that can promote expertise
- **Externally hosted blog collectives** that may have a group of frequent contributors, who lessen the load on any one individual
- **Professional blogs** with academic commentary on sites such as *The Guardian*, *The Economist* or *The Conversation*, which feature work by professional academics and merge journalism and academia into group blogs
- **Individual blogs** that can be set up online in an hour for free, unlike more complex websites. The single-author blog fits researchers and knowledge workers who are committed to writing relatively often. They often include both personal and professional reflections.

An alternative can be individual bloggers who may choose to post on existing platforms such as LinkedIn rather than have a separate site.

Content and frequency

Pretty much any sort of content can be used on blogs, including useful tools such as interactive data visualisations. Likewise, the look, style of writing and authoritative voice can vary enormously.

One piece of guidance that flows across this fluid world is the need to post content regularly. How often you are able to do that will depend on your other commitments and whether you are going for short, sharp blogs; much longer, in-depth work; something in between; or all of the above.

Uses of blogs

- **Research**. Unlike peer-reviewed journal articles that have long publishing timeframes, blogs can provide instant ongoing commentary and conversations about your thinking, approach to challenges, interim findings and the progress of your work. The more insightful and interactive you are, the more likely you are to garner an active following

- **Explainers and guides**. Demystify complex areas and expand your audience

- **Reaching practitioners and policymakers**. What are the practical applications of your work? How might you influence the narrative around issues? What does your analysis show?

- **Current affairs commentary**. Some disciplines like economics lend themselves to commenting on events in real time

- **Event commentary**. Reporting on events such as conferences can provide useful summaries and highlight insights gained.

46 Mollett, A, Brumley, C, Gilson, C & Williams, S 2017, *Communicating Your Research with Social Media: A Practical Guide to Using Blogs, Podcasts, Data Visualisations and Video*, Sage Publishing, London.
47 Ibid

CHAPTER 29

PowerPoints

- An information dump or enhancement of your script?

- Your images must support your narration

- Minimise text on slides if you don't want to lose your audience

- Presentations and handouts: consider two different sets of slides

- Ensure consistent style, engaging slides and have a backup on the day

Slide presentations tend to cover the full spectrum from highly engaging to stymying presentations with the proverbial 'death by PowerPoint'.

Quite a few academics still use slide decks (PowerPoints) as places to dump information rather than as enhancements to their spoken words.

Consider a presentation during which the audience becomes increasingly stressed while trying to absorb highly detailed slides and listen to the speaker. In the end many find it easier to just switch off because the conflict between what is being heard and seen becomes overwhelming.

One of the first things television reporters learn is the importance of ensuring that images strengthen the narration, rather than fight it by showing something irrelevant to the audio.

A broadcast reporter also knows we talk at roughly three words per second. So there's no sense in loading up a slide with sixty words when you are only going to talk to it for several seconds. You are more likely to end up hiding your key points in the blur of words.

❝ *The test is not to see how much text fits into a space – but how much of a concept you can stick into the brain.* **❞**

DIANNA BOOHER, *AUTHOR, WHAT MORE CAN I SAY?*[48]

What's the purpose of your slide deck?

Is your slide deck going to be used as a handout or part of a presentation? Detailed slides may work as handouts to be read, but those slides may need heavy modification to effectively accompany a talk. However, you may find a presentation with just images on several slides does not work as a handout. You can try to strike a balance between the two but it's often easier to have each set of slides tailored for its specific purpose.

Is your presentation for an in-person talk or a webinar? During an in-person talk the audience will be looking at you, your slides and whatever else is of interest around the room. During a webinar they are only looking at the slides, with possibly a tiny 'you' talking in the corner of the screen. Therefore, you usually need more slides in a webinar to keep up the momentum. If a single slide is up for too long, it can feel like the PowerPoint presentation is stuck.

Things to consider when creating a slide deck

Less is definitely more. It's better to have a few compelling slides than have people lose concentration.

It's a visual medium so make it visually compelling. Look for the more surprising and engaging images. Avoid unnecessary, generic or meaningless images, and pictures that don't support the spoken words.

Stay in style. Ensure there is a consistent style of fonts, colours and formatting through your presentation. Slide decks with loads of cut-and-pasted content can look horribly messy and unprofessional. There will be times when a conference organiser will ask you to use the conference PowerPoint template, which may leave little room for your content on each slide. Even in that situation, maintain your consistency of style and break up your content to cover more slides, or cut back your content.

Do not overload slides with words. Keep it concise, clean and simple. The slide is not supposed to feature everything you want to say. A reasonable rule of thumb is no text smaller than 24-point font, although some argue for a 30-point font minimum. No more than three bullet points per slide is recommended.

Do not put up very detailed charts, overly complex diagrams or tables of statistics. Don't put up something on the assumption you can talk through what it means. Distil the key points on the slides and save the details for the handout. If you have to say 'I know you can't read this', then why are you putting up the slide?

Simplify numbers and percentages as much as possible. Figures should punch, not be ponderous.

Use visual effects sparingly. Just because you can do cool transitions between slides and other special effects does not mean you should. Overuse of effects can be distracting and look like you are opting for novelty over authority.

❝ *The next time you're faced with this more-is-better temptation, squelch the urge to splurge. Communicate more with less. Subtract to add.* **❞**

DIANNA BOOHER, *AUTHOR, WHAT MORE CAN I SAY?*[49]

Always have a backup handy if you have embedded a video into the PowerPoint or intend to link to online content. For some reason this seems to be where gremlins play most. They are less able to cause havoc if you have a backup plan with the video file available separately

213

on the computer and screenshots of whatever you want to show through the online link.

Export a PDF of your presentation and take it with the PowerPoint file. Sometimes the technology does not want to play in one format but may be fine in another. One of life's many mysteries.

When requested, do send PowerPoint presentations ahead of an event. Turning up and handing over a portable drive five minutes before your talk is stressful for the event organisers. It's also wise to request time to road test the presentation before you speak.

48 Booher, D. 2015. *What More Can I Say? Why Communication Fails and What to Do About It*. Prentice Hill Press.
49 Ibid

It's better to have a few compelling slides than have people lose concentration.

CHAPTER 30

Mentioning memes

- Just what is a contemporary meme?

- How to use these powerful, fast communications

- Memes can reach millions globally

Memes may seem like a relatively recent invention, but they are not. Pre-internet memes came in the guise of political cartoons and satirical illustrations whereas today's memes include hashtags, videos, still images with captions and infographics.

> ❝ *Internet memes as we know them are anything that can be replicated, remixed or reapplied to convey a particular sentiment.* ❞
>
> **TARENEH AZAR**, *THE MEME IS THE MESSAGE*[50]

Today memes are one of the most frequently used and powerful forms of quick communication that can be shared rapidly to reach millions globally. Many employ humour and images to make a point and convey layers of meaning in simplified forms. However, it's worth remembering that memes often speak largely to those 'in the know' so you may struggle with a meme's message if you're not part of the in-crowd.

There's no magic formula for what makes a meme go viral but it's worth considering how you might express yourself using the meme as one of the tools in your communications kit.

> ❝ *In the past, people wrote reports. Today, we share memes. Look at how you communicate: emojis in texts, images in email, and videos posted to Instagram, Facebook, or YouTube. We communicate using the shorthand of images.[51]* ❞
>
> **LARRY JORDAN**, *TECHNIQUES OF VISUAL PERSUASION*[51]

---

50 Azar, T. 2021. *The Meme is the Message.* Accessed at https://www. thememessage.com/ on 5 Oct 2021
51 Larry Jordan. 2020. *Techniques of Visual Persuasion: Create powerful images that motivate.* (Voices That Matter). Pearson.

CHAPTER 31

Visualising data

- How to instantly communicate your data

- Think visualisations and infographics

- What's your goal and what are your messages?

- Remember that less is more

- Check these design principles

Like all images, data visualisations can move beyond language to explain data in instantly understandable ways.

Charts, graphs and interactive forms of mapping all fall into the data visualisation camp, while infographics are a subset that aim to tell a story using images, icons, illustrations and charts or graphs.

Think before creation

As with all communications, you need to start with clarity about what you want to achieve and what messages or messages you want to convey.

Data visualisations should not be included if their sole purpose is to break up blocks of text.

Once you've decided you do need to visualise your data, then work out what dataset or selected statistics will best support your goals.

It is equally important to identify the data you don't need. Nothing detracts from a key message faster than drowning it in unnecessary information.

A clear message spread across a few charts is much better than a muddled message crammed, with excruciating detail, into one chart... When it comes to charts and text, less is more!

LARRY JORDAN, *TECHNIQUES OF VISUAL PERSUASION*[52]

Considerations

Whether you choose to go with a table, map, charts, graph, infographic or another form of data visualisation will depend on several factors including:

- Whether your story is based on a message or data
- The data literacy of your audience
- The type of data – are you using numbers, text or both?
- The tone and style of the publication or online site in which the visualisation will be used
- Resources available. Do you have a team member who can design graphics or interactive maps or the budget to hire a professional? If not, could you use a free service like Infogram, Canva, Piktochart or Tableau Public to build the visualisation yourself?
- How much time do you have available? Do you have time to make several charts, graphs or infographics, or just one or two?

A few design principles

- Only use what is essential. Cut back on noise and clutter. Avoid decoration. Make the key message the hero
- Highlight your key messages. Don't make the viewer work hard to understand your meaning
- Label visuals to enhance understanding of what they represent. Just calling them figure 1, figure 2 etc doesn't do much to enlighten your audience
- If you have a style guide, use it. This will provide brand style, tone, colours, fonts and logos

- Use colour thoughtfully. Remember some colours have symbolic overtones so, for example, if would be unwise to use green to represent a fossil fuel such as coal
- Use colour consistently across visuals. You don't want to end up with an unprofessional mess.

Sharing on social media

Data visualisations can be perfect for social media sharing. Therefore consider sizing the visuals to meet the requirements of different platforms and maximise the value and reach of your work.

52 Larry Jordan. 2020. *Techniques of Visual Persuasion: Create powerful images that motivate.* (Voices That Matter). Pearson.

CHAPTER 32

Still pictures

- How images can cut through and make a connection

- Why you should think laterally about unusual images

- Yes, size does count

- Know the three main picture formats

Images can provide your best chance to cut through the information-saturated environment and reach your audience, often with a stronger emotional connection.

But there are a few, simple guidelines that can make all the difference.

What will attract your audience?

First of all, think about what you are trying to say and who are you talking to. Remember that a camera lens acts as the viewer's eye to a world. What world do you want others to see?

With a photo, don't rely on any accompanying text to do the heavy lifting, because potential readers may not get to your pearls of prose if you haven't chosen the right picture to capture their attention.

Images, like words, can become cliched so it's often worth the extra effort to find the less obvious, more impactful options. Think a bit laterally about what may work. For example, you may find something really interesting online through your state library or other institutions. However, always check the copyright on still or moving images as you may need to clear their use for your purposes.

No excuse for poor quality

Today, in this age of high-quality, smart phone cameras and reputable websites that do not charge for royalty-free still images – like unsplash.com and pexels.com – there really isn't much excuse for using pictures of dubious quality.

Always aim to collect images of the highest resolution. As with video, you can save a still image in a lower resolution format, but you can't miraculously make a low resolution picture higher.

Size counts

Also understand that different platforms use different-sized formats. For example, Twitter and LinkedIn tend to use images no larger than 5MB and with dimensions of around 1024 pixels by 512 px.

Online services like Canva, which has free and paid versions, will size images to fit specific platforms. However, if you frequently use a certain size image and can remember the dimensions you want, it's easy enough to resize a picture directly on your computer.

Fiddling with formats

The other basic need-to-know is the difference between a TIFF, JPEG and PNG image. (There are other formats but we'll let you hunt those down yourselves.)

- **JPEG**: This is the most commonly used format. JPEG (Joint Photographic Experts Group) provides a compressed picture of relatively small size. With a .jpg image you are trading speed and ease of use for quality

- **TIFF**: Tagged Image File Format images, which end in .tif, are very high quality but are not compressed. This means they can be very large, which makes them unsuitable for a number of purposes including fast uploads on the web

- **PNG**: Portable Network Graphics or PNGs were originally designed for use on the web. They are close to TIFF images in quality and will maintain the sharpness of highly complex images. PNGs are also particularly good if you want a transparent background – especially if placing logos on top of pictures.

First of all, think about what you are
trying to say and who are you talking to?
Remember that a camera lens acts as the
viewer's eye to a world. What world do
you want others to see?

CHAPTER 33

Moving pictures

- Why you need to really plan your video shoots

- Key points to check before you start filming

- How long will it take? Probably at least double your estimate

- Back up everything in three different places

- Lousy sound will kill your video

This will sound like telling you how to suck eggs, but moving pictures NEED TO MOVE.

During filming or in the edit, there is only so much panning across, pulling out, zooming in, tilting up, tilting down and pulling focus that you can do before being seasick feels like a more desirable option than continuing to watch the video.

The best way to get great moving pictures is to film something that moves. More often than not, that requires planning.

This means being clear on what you want to achieve, the assets you already have and what needs to be videoed. The more you think about this, the better it will be for a production crew to ensure they have the right equipment for the job and are set to film at optimal times.

For example, if you want to film two people walking and talking, that may take certain types of wireless microphones, a dolly for the camera and ensuring the light at the location will work.

Even when you are filming something yourself, the more you think about the possible scenarios, the more effectively you are likely to plan. For example, it's always a good idea to check the Bureau of Meteorology radar on the BOM app to ensure it's not about to rain when you are starting an interview outside.

Also, think about changing light, moving shadows and intermittent noises. These can mean parts of the video won't match up if you want to edit between different sections.

A few other pointers (based on unfortunate experiences) to keep in mind:

Never assume the people with whom you are filming understand what you need

Even if they say they are familiar with working with camera crews, double check. There's no point in turning up with the meter ticking on a freelance camera crew only to find the people you want to film have knocked off for lunch, are busy in a meeting or think they'll only need to be there for a jiffy.

Never assume people will understand how long filming can take

Let's face it, who in their right mind would expect to be filmed doing the same basic movement from three or even four different angles? Oh, and did we mention the drone shot we wanted as well? Suggesting people double or triple the time they think filming will take often seems to work quite well. Always best to have agreement on the worst possible scenario and then finish early.

The other end of the timing scenario is when the news camera crew and journalist scream in the door like their pants are on fire, film you answering three quick questions, grab the gear and run out again leaving a cloud of dust, from where they had hurriedly rearranged your furniture, in their wake.

Always back up everything

Video takes up loads of space so plan for terabytes of storage and have portable hard drives handy. Some may call it paranoia, but it can't be stressed enough how nothing digital is safe unless it's stored in three different places. Back up, back up and back up again. With a laptop there is often nothing to stop you backing up the first part of a shoot while the camera person is videoing the next bit of vision.

Logistics can be key

Sort out a system to label files. A lot of video production is about good organisation. Get your process down and stick with it. It will save editing time. It is also surprising how often you may want to go back and find something filmed ages ago.

You paid for it, so make sure you get all the source vision

If you hire a production team, ensure the dubbing and supply of the raw vision on a portable hard drive is costed in, along with you receiving the finished edited product. You never know when you will want the unedited vision in the future. It's really annoying when the only vision you have has a nice song and no sound effects, thereby making it nigh on impossible to re-purpose later.

It's not all about the images

As the video editing expert, Larry Jordan says: 'The best way to improve the quality of your picture is to improve the quality of your sound.'[53] You can do wonders to improve vision in the edit suite but if the sound is lousy, it will be unwatchable.

Sound quality is crucial and that usually means using a microphone that is external to your camera. Don't rely on the microphone built into your phone or camera. Those microphones may be okay for sound effects of machines or whatever but they won't cut it with longer interviews (although you may get away with using them for short social media posts).

> 66 *Nothing turns people off faster than bad audio. People will happily watch bad video – YouTube is the ultimate proof of this – but they will never listen to bad audio.* 99

LARRY JORDAN, *VIDEO EDITING EXPERT*[54]

53 Larry Jordan. 2020. *Techniques of Visual Persuasion: Create powerful images that motivate.* (Voices That Matter). Pearson.
54 Ibid

CHAPTER 34

Podcasting possibilities

- How and why podcasts can really work

- Tips and tricks for creating podcasts

- Google is your 'how to' friend

- Build your audience by scheduling episodes

- Share findings and data in early-stage research

The rise and rise of podcasts is an interesting phenomenon when so much of the world now consumes information largely via video.

For the listener, podcasts provide the opportunity to learn while doing other things – and there's a lot to be said for not having to stare constantly at a screen. They can also provide an immersive, intimate experience as they inspire listeners to create images in their minds.

For beginners, audio can be less scary than working with video because you don't have to worry about pictures as well as sound. However, the two do not need to be mutually exclusive because you can use audio taken from a video to create podcasts. (See the example of a digital story process on page 235).

Another advantage of audio-only focus is that nervous interviewees often find audio-recording much less daunting than being on camera (although, with experience, you can learn how to make just about anyone feel at ease in any medium).

What constitutes a podcast?

A podcast is essentially an edited audio file that is uploaded to a platform on the internet. From there the file (usually in mp3 format) can be downloaded on to computers or portable devices like phones for easy listening.

Listeners can subscribe to specific podcasts so they will automatically receive new episodes or shows.

Successful podcasts can quickly build audiences of millions of subscribers worldwide.

Nothing is too niche for a podcast. If you are interested in a particular area, there's every chance that others are too.

Low barriers to entry

Podcasts can be inexpensive and less technical to make than you may think.

Becoming a podcaster requires only an audio recorder (which could be your phone), a microphone and free software, like Audacity or Garageband.

Many highly successful podcasters have experimented and learned how to work most efficiently and effectively by Googling 'how to' instructions and then building their skills through practical experience.

The alternative is to hire professionals if your ambitions surpass your podcasting skills. Some universities may have experts, a studio and equipment available, or you can hire external producers.

Whatever you do, start by being clear on why you want to podcast, what you want to say and who you want to reach.

Degrees of difficulty

From lowest to highest degrees of difficulty, a podcast may be:

- Just one person talking, as in a monologue, lecture or another type of presentation
- A conversation or interview with two people
- Multiple interviews edited together to cover a specific subject or theme
- Full-scale lengthy productions with multiple voices, sound effects, music and some seriously schmick editing.

> *"Podcasts from academic and research organisations...are becoming increasingly varied as universities and funding bodies invest more in diverse forms of dissemination in order to react to audience trends and interests."*
>
> COMMUNICATING YOUR RESEARCH WITH SOCIAL MEDIA[55]

Building podcasting into your work

Podcasts can be incorporated into your daily or weekly workflow or scheduled to provide insight into different stages of research.

As Mollett et al say:'We can easily imagine podcasts created at the final stages of your project as part of the communications strategy or content dissemination, but academics and researchers in all fields have many opportunities to share findings and data at those early stages too.'[56]

'The idea of broadcasting the building blocks of your research so early on may be somewhat off-putting, especially for early-career academics sensitive to criticism, but there are many potential rewards and opportunities that spring from starting podcasting near the beginning of the Research Lifecycle.'

Sharing your podcasts

Podcast content platforms – like Soundcloud, Apple Podcasts, Spotify, Google Podcasts, Audible and many others – have their own ways of distributing content. You can use those platforms to host your podcasts and also use their link to your content on your website.

55 Mollett, A, Brumley, C, Gilson C & Williams, S. 2017, *Communicating Your Research with Social Media: A Practical Guide to Using Blogs, Podcasts, Data Visualisations and Video*, Sage Publishing, London.
56 Ibid

PROCESS FOR CREATION OF VIDEO STORIES WITH TEXT AND AUDIO OFFSHOOTS FILES

CONCEPT
Identify issues to be highlighted and story or stories to tell, with reference to your communications strategy

↓

RESEARCH
Collate background information, locations and other visual materials to support the stories. Identify those who will tell the stories and their availability.

↓

BRIEF
Provide brief to producer that includes objectives, research, technical requirements, timelines, deliverables and who will be responsible for approving different stages of the project

↓

OUTLINE AND QUOTE
Based on the brief, producer prepares video outline and quote for pre-production (setting up shoot); production (videoing all components); and post-production (scripting, editing and deliverables)

↓

APPROVE
Outline and quote

↓

PRE-PRODUCTION
Schedule videoing of interviews and other story components. Ensure vision already shot and/or music to be used in either videos or podcasts have copyright clearance

↓

PRODUCTION
Video story components and log shots during filming. Digitise any still images in highest possible resolution

↓

EDIT
Ingest all vision into editing system

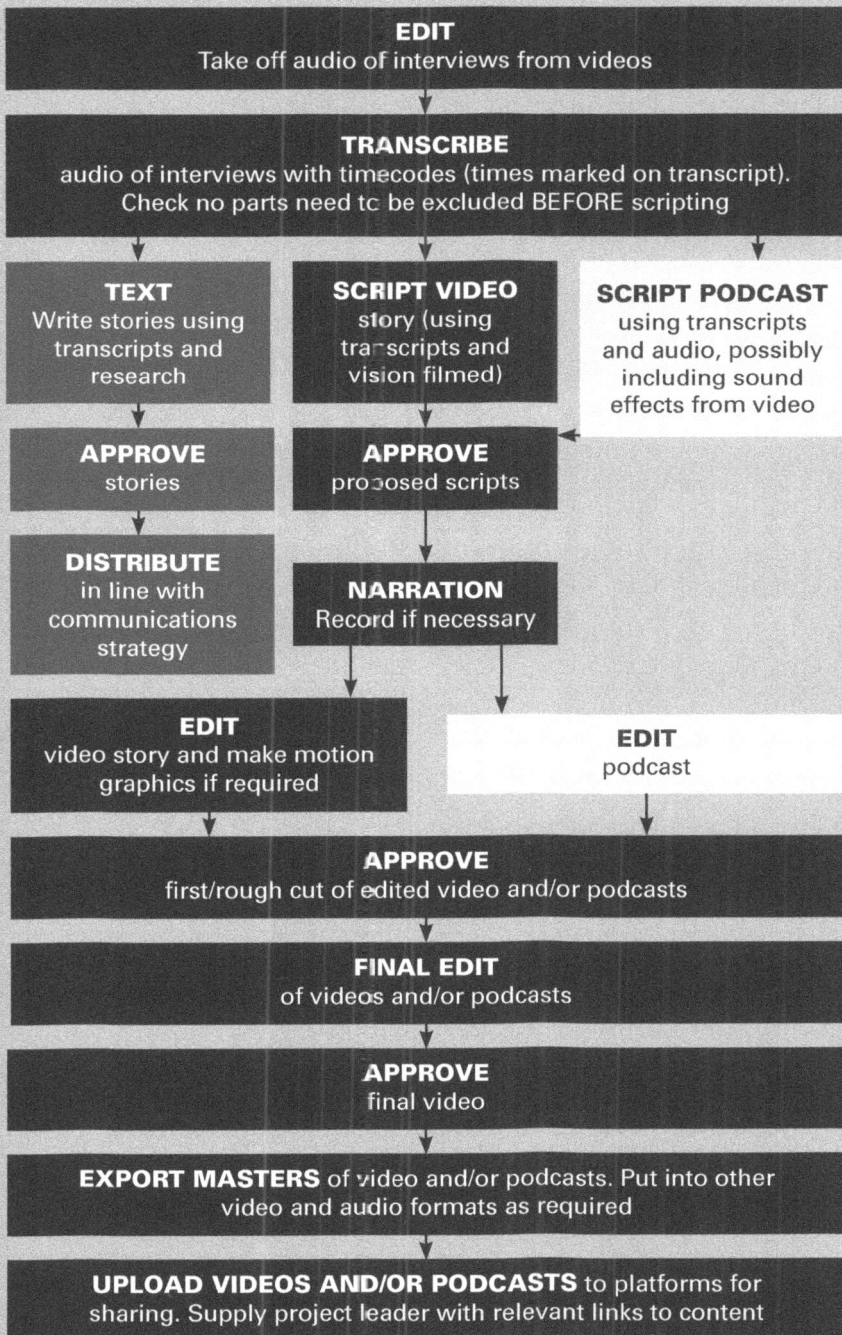

EDIT
Take off audio of interviews from videos

TRANSCRIBE
audio of interviews with timecodes (times marked on transcript).
Check no parts need to be excluded BEFORE scripting

TEXT
Write stories using transcripts and research

SCRIPT VIDEO
story (using transcripts and vision filmed)

SCRIPT PODCAST
using transcripts and audio, possibly including sound effects from video

APPROVE
stories

APPROVE
proposed scripts

DISTRIBUTE
in line with communications strategy

NARRATION
Record if necessary

EDIT
video story and make motion graphics if required

EDIT
podcast

APPROVE
first/rough cut of edited video and/or podcasts

FINAL EDIT
of videos and/or podcasts

APPROVE
final video

EXPORT MASTERS of video and/or podcasts. Put into other video and audio formats as required

UPLOAD VIDEOS AND/OR PODCASTS to platforms for sharing. Supply project leader with relevant links to content

6

Strategically sharing your work

CHAPTER 35

Preparing to be newsworthy

- Exactly what do you have to offer?

- Here's a good way to test your pitch

- What makes the best pitch?

- Tips for being newsworthy

- How to touch a nerve

Before approaching any journalist or media organisation, you need to be clear on what you have to offer. This usually requires preparation in distilling your information, clarifying your message and knowing what you want to achieve.

Simplifying messages can take a good deal of effort but it also helps improve your focus and is rarely time wasted.

As a test, imagine what your pitch may need if it is to cut through to a newsroom chief of staff who has several television stations running on monitors around the desk and is dealing with an office of reporters and camera crews, constantly changing news stories, endless media releases, emails and a phone that won't stop ringing.

What makes a good pitch?

A pitch is not all about you and your work. It should be about what you can offer the person or people you are trying to persuade or interest.

The worst pitches are barked at people. Who likes being told what they should be doing or how they should feel?

The best pitches are underpinned by a clear view of the audience's interests, needs and wants, and how you and your work can benefit them. Good pitches are conversations that interest, educate, energise and inspire action.

❝Pitching – whether a formal sales pitch, an elevator pitch, or a crafted commercial – causes people to duck. A conversation, on the other hand, invites them to engage and exchange information. If you intend to persuade, make sure you're conversing, not pitching. Keep the discussion two directional. ❞

DIANE BOOHER, *AUTHOR, WHAT MORE CAN I SAY?*[57]

Preparing to be newsworthy

Being timely is often a key attraction for media.

Some people keep on top of industry, sector and more general public affairs because it's part of their job.

Economist Warren Hogan finds it easy to be relevant because he is working on the performance of the economy, 'which has offshoots into policy and forecasting and a whole lot of things people generally find interesting.'

'The core of it is me sitting there looking at the economies day in, day out and trying to work out, as best we can, what's going on. And, of course, that's high frequency and high interest in terms of the media.'

Professor Hogan says academics working in other areas may find it more difficult to capture media interest but that doesn't mean they shouldn't try.

If your area of expertise does not require keeping a finger on the pulse of the nation, you can still look for ways to add insight to current and future issues and events.

For example, you may keep some written background handy so when your research becomes particularly relevant to a newsworthy event or issue, you only need write the first part of an article which directly addresses the event or issue, and you are ready with a timely opinion piece, blog or story. It's much easier to be speedy in your response if you have already prepared a large part of the work.

You can also keep your ear to the ground and think how your research could forge stronger connections with current or unfolding events.

Serendipity or making your own luck?

The University of Sydney Business School's Marian Baird moved swiftly from focusing on one issue to looking more broadly at women's working lives.

'I often wonder about did I just happen to be the right person at the right time? This whole interest in women and work, getting women back into the workforce and the ageing workforce is what I'm doing now.

'I suppose you create your own luck. But I am very careful to listen to what the journalists are asking questions about because, I think, that does give us a little bit of a sense of that's where the movement of interest is going,' Professor Baird says.

Riding the wave

Steve Worthington of Swinburne Business School feels lucky to have landed on a topic with lots of longevity and twists and turns.

"You find a wave, you get on it. You ride it as far as you can, and then it falls away. You look around for the next wave.

'I started off looking at payment cards and all kinds of store cards, like Myer and David Jones. But now I'm moving on a little bit towards financial fraud. So I'm not really getting off this wave, but I'm looking for other waves as well,' Professor Worthington says.

Touching a nerve

66 If you can find a research topic that really hits a nerve, you're always going to get to be able to get stuff published. 99

ELIZABETH SHEEDY, MACQUARIE BUSINESS SCHOOL

Elizabeth Sheedy of Macquarie Business School has found great interest in her research on executive remuneration.

'I guess it's not too surprising that a lot of people are really angered by some of the CEO salaries (probably, in my view, a little bit disproportionately). So the extent of the anger sometimes surprises me a bit. But I guess, in a way, that creates an opportunity,' Professor Sheedy says.

Curtin Business School's Steven Rowley used to focus on the commercial property sector, but moved more into housing which had a higher likelihood of funding and impact.

'If you want to advance your career, well that's what you do. You have to chase, quite frankly, that funding and chase those areas where you think you may be able to make a difference,' he says.

A PhD in what?

People have laughed when Louise Grimmer of UTAS Business School has told them about her PhD in retailing. Some of the things she writes and talks about are not life changing or world saving but, Dr Grimmer says, 'we are talking about topics that do impact our daily lives and the people who work in retail and service industries.'

For example, a topic like Christmas shopping may seem trivial but it affects a lot of people and businesses. It's also a topic which many consumer media cover every year. 'Small

businesses employ a lot of people. Retailing is the second largest employing sector in the country,' Dr Grimmer says.

Getting a jump on the news

Another way of ensuring you can provide a timely response is to think about which major reports are coming down the line.

Journalists are often given embargoed copies of reports so they can have their stories ready to go when the report is released. You can seek an embargoed copy so you are ready to comment as soon as the embargo is lifted at a specific date and time.

If you can't get an embargoed copy from the organisation behind the report or find a copy that 'has fallen off the back of a truck', then a journalist with whom you have a trusting relationship may be happy to share the report. This may be done with the understanding that you wouldn't say who gave you the report, would not break the embargo and would be ready to provide insightful comments when the report is released.

As an aside, each year on the day before the evening release of state and federal government budgets, journalists go into a budget lockup. They are cut off from the outside world, given time to analyse the documents and prepare their articles and commentary. They are released from the lockup when the Treasurer gets up to make the budget speech in the evening.

Stakeholders may also apply to the government to attend a lockup so they too are across the detailed budget papers. This may be of interest to academics able to justify why they should be in a lockup.

---

57 Booher, D. 2015. *What More Can I Say? Why Communication Fails and What to Do About It*. Prentice Hill Press.

CHAPTER 36

Targeting media outlets

- How to reach a broader audience

- Will your industry partners be comfortable with your media approach?

- Be ready to talk to all media

- Look for specialist publications

If you are on top of current issues and events in your area, you probably already have a reasonable idea of where your potential audiences get their information. However, if you want to reach wider groups you may need to broaden your search and/or seek advice from your university communications team or other communications professionals.

"Always understand media is about audience. "

CATHERINE WEBBER, *BOND UNIVERSITY*

It can be argued that there is no such thing as the *general public*, however there are media outlets that reach a very broad and diverse range of people while others serve clearly definable niche audiences.

Those you want to reach may also get information from less public but highly credible sources such as newsletters. Organisational publications are often very pleased to have good, fresh, credible content to share with their distribution lists.

Signalling media intentions up front

So there are no surprises, Macquarie Business School's Elizabeth Sheedy ensures she is very clear with industry partners about the extent of her media work.

She can't always present things in a way that is going to make partners comfortable, and some people are not willing to be involved on that basis.

'So it does cut off some opportunities to do research – I think we need to be honest about that – but I can't allow my research to be controlled by an industry partner. Otherwise, it's not really research, it's consulting,' Professor Sheedy says.

Going wide

Carl Rhodes of UTS Business School recommends looking broadly at mainstream, independent and citizen journalism and international outlets that accept unsolicited submissions. Some outlets have a small but highly specialised distribution and may be good places for early career researchers to start.

'I would also advise people to pay attention to what they read, because these days we don't just read the magazine we go and buy or the newspaper we go and buy. We read the stuff that kind of comes to us through social media,' Professor Rhodes says.

The University of Sydney Business School's Marian Baird says certain socioeconomic groups talk to each other through certain media outlets and, 'if we are serious about our research and we think it's important to Australia, we have to be able to talk to everyone.

'So you have to be on talkback radio. You have to be on something other than the ABC. You have to be in something other than *The Age* or the *Sydney Morning Herald* or the *Financial Review*,' she says.

'You need to be in the more general outlets as well. So I relish it when I get a call from those outlets.' Professor Baird also likes talking to regional outlets as they can sometimes provide more time to explore topics with the public and are a means of strengthening regional connections with academics.

Going to industry and practitioners

Tim Harcourt of UTS Business School says: 'In the media world of today, TV and radio and newspapers can be hard work unless something is controversial. But going for specialist online publications is actually better value – they have credibility and you can get your message to a wider audience who will find your research useful.'

Swinburne Business School's Jason Pallant says he accepts requests from special publications which are read by research partners.

'I will say *yes* to any *Inside Retail* request that comes in because I know it's directly relevant and also, from experience, I know that they value data and research and insights,' Dr Pallant says.

Gary Mortimer of QUT Business School works with industry media on more targeted approaches but goes with traditional mainstream media to reach broader audiences.

However, he says: 'Interestingly enough, I've had a lot of contact from CEOs and MDs wanting me to come and speak to their industry groups, to do keynote speeches as a result of maybe a comment I've made on the news media, on *The Project, Today Show* or *Sunrise*'.

Crossover publications

Crossover journals – like *Harvard Business Review* and *MIT's Sloan Management Review* – are also well worth considering as they have prestige, credibility and high international circulation.

CHAPTER 37

Scattergun or exclusivity?

- Hit many targets or aim at one?

- Put a time limit on exclusives

- Know your media and target them

- Be careful of favouring a few

On top of deciding who to approach, you need to work out the best way to distribute your message. There are broadly two main choices with variations in between.

Scattergun: This involves sending a media release or alert to all and sundry either using your own contact list or through an organisation that distributes media releases for a fee. The aim is to hit as many targets as possible in the hope that some will use your story.

Exclusives: Here you offer your story to only one journalist or media outlet. Journalists obviously like being the recipient of exclusives and may invest time and energy into creating a great exclusive story.

The downside is the potential for you to annoy the other journalists, particularly on a specialist round, if you frequently play favourites.

That aside, it is always worth offering an exclusive for a defined period of time. Otherwise you can end up with a media organisation stalling on using it for any number of internal reasons, while you are left with no media coverage and the inability to offer the story elsewhere.

A journalist's perspective

When discussing the scattergun approach, journalist Peter Ryan bemoans PR departments that 'spam chiefs of staff and news desks rather than targeting people who are actually interested' because the information may never be passed to the right person.

He says: 'You've got to have your list of people who you know are interested, and don't just email them, but ring them up and say, *Hey, I've got this coming up. I thought you might be interested. We can give you an embargo*'.

Being scooped

Campus Morning Mail editor, Stephen Matchett, loathes being scooped. 'I hate it. Does my audience care? Probably not that much. Will they remember? No. My job is to report the news, and if I'm not reporting the news, I'm not doing the job,' he says.

Matchett actively works to report higher education news not covered elsewhere. 'I contemplated having a slug for *the news you won't read anywhere else* but, for obvious reasons, that is very high risk. I think that's what I try and do. It's not a question of me getting a spin on it at all. It's a question of just getting it out there. All news is important to someone.'

John Ross of *Times Higher Education* says he becomes frustrated with himself but will admire a journalist 'who's just worked harder, has good contacts and has got close to the story'.

'All power to them and, if I'm piggybacking on the reporting they've done, I would usually cite them. I'd definitely cite them if they're the only person who's reported it so far. So it's not an annoyance, it's more like a bit of self-flagellation to make yourself work harder.

'I guess where I get annoyed is where the playing field is not level, and that's often the case with political stuff where they just drop to the favoured few and others miss out. That's just annoying. It happens all the time,' Ross says.

Bravely exclusive

The ABC's Conor Duffy is an advocate for people being brave enough to give a story to only one journalist. 'For most stories you're probably better off going with one person because they'll be able to invest time in your story rather than getting a media release hours before an embargo lifts. Good journalists do their own work and their own sort of investigations to tease out those ideas.'

But Duffy agrees with having a deadline on the exclusivity. He says: 'Maybe give people a week beyond what they've said because news cycles do fluctuate. Sometimes if I've got a good story I will hold it for a couple of days, because I know that when the Liberal Party spill or whatever is out of the news cycle, there's going to be a lot more space for it. But yeah, some journalists will, if they think they can get away with it, just have it sit on the shelf for way too long. So I think you just need to be firm and clear and say, *We're giving this to you exclusively. Run it or give it up.*'

Duffy adds you can also put out a wider media release after an exclusive story has run, which would probably be picked up in a number of places.

*Good journalists do their own work
and their own sort of investigations*

7

Connecting with social media

CHAPTER 38

Why use social media?

- Understand the positives and negatives of social media

- Which platforms are right for you?

- Clear, concise and short posts have the biggest impact

- How much time should you invest?

- How to boost engagement with your research via social media

Social media offer a speedy, exciting world of heightened visibility, spreadability, interaction and collaboration. They are tools for communication and building online communities that can be huge – or serving only those with niche interests.

Social media are an effective way to promote your expertise and work.

“ *This does not just include the promotion of articles and research; it also means participating (though not always) in social media discussions in areas of their research and on current events and general societal trends.* **”**

COMMUNICATING YOUR RESEARCH WITH SOCIAL MEDIA[58]

Social media can take you around the traditional gatekeepers of institutions, mainstream media and academic publishing to rapidly reach many people within your areas of interest and well beyond.

Needless to say, the possibility of widespread positive and negative responses to you and your communications can be unnerving; there are dangers like vicious trolls on the attack or you saying things that could later come back to bite you. There is also the potential problem of becoming part of an echo chamber in which there is a lack of diversity of views.

But many academics find that the risk of using social media is far outweighed by its potential rewards.

“ *Digital technology lowers barriers to publication while also making it easier to search what is out there. There are far more publications grappling for our attention and for this reason, increasing numbers of academics take action to ensure their publications are visible.* **”**

MARK CARRIGAN, *AUTHOR OF SOCIAL MEDIA FOR ACADEMICS*[59]

Changing from controlled exposure to mixing with the masses

We don't underestimate the mind shift required to engage outside more controlled and familiar environments, and the challenge of sustaining a social media presence that achieves your goals. Indeed, the more practical side of learning to use each social media platform may be the easiest part.

The real challenge lies in deciding which platform or platforms may be of most use to you; ensuring they connect well with your work and audiences; and assessing if you have the time, smarts and energy to sustain your social media presence.

> *Sustainability is key because the benefits of social media tend to accrue with time rather than being immediate.*
>
> **MARK CARRIGAN,** *AUTHOR OF SOCIAL MEDIA FOR ACADEMICS*[60]

As Mark Carrigan points out, it is better to be on one platform frequently with posts and responses than it is to spread yourself too thinly over several social media platforms.

'Once you find what works for you, stick with it. There's no need to be active on all platforms, and doing so could easily detract from your capacity to derive any satisfaction or enjoyment from a single one of them,' he says.

It's also worth considering if you are better off becoming a member of a group where the workload is shared by others also contributing to blogs and additional platforms.

Many degrees of engagement

Online media engagement can be as simple as establishing a Google Scholar profile to make your work more easily discoverable, keeping your personal and institutional webpages up to date, setting up a LinkedIn profile or joining a group like academic.edu and ResearchGate to share research.

The middle ground could be building an email list and using emails to directly promote a new piece of work such as a report or sending out a newsletter. (Services like Mailchimp and Campaign Monitor can be of great assistance here).

"Rather than blurring the boundaries between the academe and journalism, I think that social media use by academics can constitute a 'third space' that mediates between them, helping those working in the media to find and make contact with academics in a way that is more likely to be mutually beneficial and informed throughout by an understanding of what the other does. "

MARK CARRIGAN, *AUTHOR OF SOCIAL MEDIA FOR ACADEMICS*[61]

The highest level of social media engagement and/or time consumed may be commenting and posting several times a day on Twitter or another platform, creating videos, or often writing blogs that are between 500 and 1500 words in length.

Social media's promotion of person-to-person engagement allows you to communicate with colleagues, students and the wider public. It also allows journalists to discover you and vice versa.

Short writing and visuals

In social media, less is almost always more.

On most platforms you can point to a longer piece of work but it's best to keep the social media communications short and pithy.

For example, on Twitter you have only 280 characters in which to convey a message. In those 280 characters, you also need to count twitter handles and hashtags. Twitter handles help your tweet to connect with relevant people or organisations – the ABDC's handle is @businessdeans.

❝ *Researchers are in a unique position on social media because we have easily verifiable credibility as authoritative voices.* **❞**

MARK REED, *AUTHOR, RESEARCH IMPACT HANDBOOK*[62]

Hashtags help people to find your tweet by providing themes like #auspol for Australian politics or #highered for higher education.

However, social media has the side benefit of honing your writing into concise, clear copy and teaching you the best ways to draw attention to your work through still or moving images. Pay attention to what others are doing and how much interaction they generate.

Assisting your research

In *Communicating Your Research with Social Media*, Mollett et al. contend that a linear model of research communication – where work is researched, published, and then (if you're lucky) disseminated outside academia – does not necessarily serve the interests of researchers and wider society. [63]

> **❝** *Given the stretched nature of researcher workloads and research budgets, getting the most out of your social and digital media activity is incredibly important.* **❞**
>
> COMMUNICATING YOUR RESEARCH WITH SOCIAL MEDIA[64]

They argue that 'the opportunities and challenges of new communication tools actually reflect the changing face of research itself.

'In this way, social and digital media can be understood less as an external burden placed on the research environment, and more as an available option for a range of modern-day research activities.'

However, they do say that social media should not be left to the end of a project, because researchers should boost their online presence to maximise engagement.

In a bid to assist you in deciding which social media may work best for you and your subject areas, we've compiled a brief overview of some of the major platforms available at the time of writing.

We also provide a glimpse of how two early career researchers have strengthened their research and teaching communication by using the platform TikTok, which is often viewed only as a place for young people to share silly videos.

58 Mollett, A, Brumley, C, Gilson, C & Williams, S. 2017. *Communicating Your Research with Social Media: A Practical Guide to Using Blogs, Podcasts, Data Visualisations and Video.* Sage Publishing, London
59 Carrigan, M. 2019 *Social Media for Academics*, (2nd edition). Sage Publishing, London.
60 Ibid
61 Ibid
62 Reed, MS. 2018, *The Research Impact Handbook*, 2nd Edition. Fast Track Impact, London.
63 Mollett, A, Brumley, C, Gilson, C & Williams, S. 2017, *Communicating Your Research with Social Media: A Practical Guide to Using Blogs, Podcasts, Data Visualisations and Video*, Sage Publishing, London
64 Ibid

Platform	What it is	What types of content can you share	Audience	Tone of Voice	Post Examples	Why use it?
LinkedIn	LinkedIn is the world's largest professionally focused social media platform with over 774 million users. LinkedIn allows its members to connect with colleagues, follow industry- and field-leaders, join groups of like-minded researchers and share research	Text-based posts up to 3000 characters long (although only the first 200 can be seen before readers are required to press 'see more') URLs Photos smaller than 5MB Videos up to 10 minutes long Live streamed videos up to four hours long	Professionals 20-60+	Professional, serious and business-like LinkedIn is for sharing your work and ideas rather than your day-to-day activities and selfies (unless at an industry-relevant event)	Best to join LinkedIn and observe the types of posts being made by your connections	LinkedIn allows you to: Connect with colleagues Join industry groups Share information Follow leaders in your field Provide others with a summary of your work history

Platform	What it is	What types of content can you share	Audience	Tone of Voice	Post Examples	Why use it?
Twitter	Twitter is a fast-moving microblogging website that aims to create and foster conversations among its 350 million + users.	Text posts (tweets) up to 280 characters long URLs Photos up to 5MB Looping GIFs up to 5MB on mobile and 15MB on web Videos up to 140 seconds long (two mins 20 sec) Audio up to 140 seconds long	Mixture of people using Twitter for professional and/or casual purposes 25-49+	Depends on who your audience is and the type of post Something related to your work should have a professional tone while jokes, fun ideas and general non-work-related content could have a more relaxed tone	The Australian Business Deans Council (@businessdeans) has an effective Twitter feed with a variety of content types All of the business academics featured in this book have effective Twitter accounts	Twitter allows you to: Share information and opinions Join in conversations Connect with colleagues and students Connect with industry leaders and organisations

Platform	What it is	What types of content can you share	Audience	Tone of Voice	Post Examples	Why use it?
Facebook	Facebook is the world's biggest social media platform with billions of users around the world. It's used by people across all age, gender and cultural demographics	Photos up to 30MB Videos up to 240min Text Posts 63206 characters long but shorter posts get more engagement URLs Live streamed video up to four hours long on mobile devices or eight hours on web	Casual, all ages but mainly 25-60+	Most Facebook posts have a clear, casual tone of voice. If sharing work, use a clear and professional tone that's not too serious	Best to join Facebook and observe the types of posts being made by your colleagues in industry-focused groups	Facebook allows you to: Create industry-focused groups where colleagues can share information and ideas Connect with students through dedicated subject pages Connect with colleagues on a personal level

Platform	What it is	What types of content can you share	Audience	Tone of Voice	Post Examples	Why use it?
Instagram	Instagram is an image-based social media network where users can share temporary stories or permanent photos	Photos up to 30MB Short video posts up to 60 seconds in length Reels up to 60 seconds long Stories up to 15 seconds long (they only last for 24 hours) Long videos uploaded via IGTV can be up to 60 minutes Live videos up to four hours long Captions on posts can be up to 2200 characters long	Casual, mainly 18-34	Photos, videos and written captions tend to be more casual in tone but should always be clear and concise	The Daily Aus (@thedailyaus) is a digital-first news service that provides summaries of the news headlines and stories of the day through short visual summaries. The outlet's posts are brightly coloured and provide valuable information that's highly shareable. The Australian Bureau of Statistics (@absstats) creates simple sharable graphics inspired by current events/ holidays using their expansive data-set.	Instagram allows you to: Share information with general audiences, students and potentially colleagues Join in conversations through stories and comments Connect with students through dedicated subject-area pages Interact with your followers in fun and engaging ways using stories, carousel posts and more

Platform	What it is	What types of content can you share	Audience	Tone of Voice	Post Examples	Why use it?
TikTok	TikTok is a rapidly growing short form video platform popular with Gen Z and younger millennials. On TikTok, users can share videos up to three mins long. One video doing well can grow your TikTok account very quickly	Videos up to three minutes in length (this may soon grow to five minutes) Live videos up to 60 minutes Captions up to 100 characters long	Casual, under 34 (mainly 16-24)	Casual, authentic tone of voice	NPR's Planet Money Podcast creates off-beat explainers about economics concepts On NTF's Part one: https://vm.tiktok.com/ZSJT1Vv5y/ Part two: https://vm.tiktok.com/ZSJT1tVLU/ On carbon offsets https://vm.tiktok.com/ZSJTJ1mdK/	TikTok allows you to: Share information with a young, general audience who are interested in learning something new Connect with colleagues

Platform	What it is	What types of content can you share	Audience	Tone of Voice	Post Examples	Why use it?
YouTube	YouTube is the world's largest community-based video streaming platform and is used by billions of people every month	Videos up to 15 minutes if your account is unverified or up to 12 hours long if your account is verified Shorts up to 60 seconds long Livestreams can go for as long as you want but are achived after 12 hours	Casual or professional depending on your audience, all ages but 18-35 watch it very frequently	Depends on who your audience is and your subject matter. You should always be clear, concise and authentic in how your present yourself	Behind the News: Australia's 2021 Census https://www.youtube.com/watch?v=GSh-vK5jj7Os Business Insider: How Polaroid Went From Celebrity Favourite To Bankruptcy https://www.youtube.com/watch?v=p07Zw_UkIWk Vox: How IKEA gets you to impulsively buy more https://www.youtube.com/watch?v=WYKUJg-MRQ7A	YouTube allows you to: Share information Interact with viewers in the comments

CHAPTER 39

Twitter

Twitter is a fast-moving micro-blogging platform best known for its ability to share short textposts up to 280 characters in length, facilitate conversations and allow peers to find and connect with one another. Photos, videos, URL links and audio clips can be shared and have the potential to go viral through hashtags, mentions and retweets (sharing) from other accounts.

Twitter is popular with academics, journalists, politicians, policymakers and researchers due to its ease of content sharing, large user base and ability to help form connections.

❝ *One of the most enjoyable aspects of Twitter can be to suddenly find yourself in dialogue with a person whose work you were discussing.* **❞**

MARK CARRIGAN, *SOCIAL MEDIA FOR ACADEMICS*[67]

For some academics, Twitter can be a valuable source of information and commentary if they follow relevant accounts.

UTS Business School's Carl Rhodes uses Twitter in a number of ways: 'Firstly, it's probably my main source of news. I don't go and buy the printed newspaper anymore. So, a lot of news that I read comes through referrals on Twitter. And I make commentary on a number of stories related to that. If I do have articles published in the media, I will tweet about them, as well as retweet other things that other people may have done.'

For some, like Louise Grimmer of UTAS Business School, Twitter has fostered professional connections.

'Twitter is my platform that I really love because I just think it really has a huge reach. It's enabled me to meet some incredible people. I met Gary Mortimer (QUT) via Twitter. I met Jason Pallant (Swinburne) via Twitter. I would not be working with those guys if it weren't for Twitter. I mean that's incredible luck. Gary and I have written 24 articles for *The Conversation*, we've published three journal articles together. And he's a friend as well.'

Twitter is also home to many journalists who will use the platform to find experts to help provide insights and/or commentary for their stories. It also works in reverse for academics wanting to contact journalists.

'That's where a journalist will go to get their insights and start writing their story. So, if you want to be seen in that way, you need to be on there,' Swinburne Business School's Jason Pallant says.

When it comes to social media, John Ross of *Times Higher Education* only engages on Twitter. He finds it useful for research and knows journalists who use it to promote their work. 'If you tweet it out to people who retweet it to a lot of people, then I think it probably has a lot of value as a distribution tool. But I think its main utility is in finding out about potential stories and getting a sense of how people feel about them, and sometimes getting very useful, specific pieces of information.'

If you are using Twitter professionally it is wise to have a clear description of your areas of expertise in your short Twitter biography. 'Father of three, lover of bush walks, mad soccer player' is not particularly helpful when a journalist or colleague is looking for someone who is an expert on corporate governance.

As Twitter is a public forum, anyone can view and interact with your content so there are times when you will need to have a thick skin.

Rae Cooper of The University of Sydney Business School says she is trolled constantly. 'If it's absolutely revolting abuse, which is quite common, I just block immediately. If it's a circumstance with someone with a high public profile, for example, a politician or something like that, I try to take the approach that if you're abusive back, nobody wins. I try to take a demeanour which is: *I would like to explain my research to you very politely.*'

There is also the fuelling of very heated debates; some toxic, others just a healthy democracy at work.

> **“** *Twitter can be dangerous in terms of the polarisation and the algorithms running it. If you choose a battle, that can really generate polarised – and some really shallow – discussion.* **”**
> **SARAH JANE KELLY,** *UQ BUSINESS SCHOOL*

Only share what you are happy to have out in the digital sphere indefinitely. There are many examples of backlash over old, problematic tweets that have tarnished reputations and damaged careers.

You also never know where your tweet may end up.

'Sometimes you put a tweet out when you're quite angry about something…and it will get picked up and embedded in the story and sometimes that's good, sometimes it's less good,' Professor Cooper says. 'One tweet that I put out ended up in *The New York Times* just because the journo happened to read the tweet that was particularly relevant to something that he was looking at on a particular day.'

Catherine Webber of Bond University says that academics shouldn't tweet if they can't just block idiots or trolls and let their comments go. However, her experience has largely been positive with Twitter as an inclusive community where laughs, tears and information are shared.

Chopping and changing won't endear you to followers

❝I don't one minute tweet something about corruption in the finance industry and then five minutes later send out a picture of my dog looking cute. ❞

PROFESSOR CARL RHODES, *UTS BUSINESS SCHOOL*

To maintain an effective Twitter account, it's important to be consistent with your content so your followers have a clear picture of what you represent.

There are a number of social media scheduling tools that allow you to post across multiple accounts and platforms. Sprout Social, Buffer and Later are all popular options and, while some like Hootsuite require a paid subscription, many offer free or low-cost versions with basic scheduling capabilities. For Twitter-only posts, TweetDeck is a free tool created by Twitter that allows you to schedule posts and keep track of feeds for multiple accounts.

The following example shows just one way of maintaining a consistent presence on the platform.

67 Carrigan, M. 2019, *Social Media for Academics*, (2nd edition). Sage Publishing, London

EXAMPLE

The ABDC uses Twitter and LinkedIn as its main social media platforms as they provide the greatest access to relevant business, media and academic audiences.

On Twitter (@businessdeans), the ABDC shares time-dependent, newsworthy content related to the higher education issues of the day and the work conducted by academics and business schools. It also shares more timeless articles from business schools around the world of interest to the wide range of business disciplines.

On LinkedIn, Leslie Falkiner-Rose ABDC Communications showcases the work of researchers from Australia's business schools and connects with students, academics, media and business leaders globally.

To maintain a consistent social media presence and save time, the ABDC uses the social media scheduler Hootsuite to pre-schedule posts for its Twitter and LinkedIn pages. The ABDC mainly pre-schedules posts that are not particularly time-sensitive, so they can be shared throughout the week to provide followers with regular interesting content. However, on busy news days, with many time-dependent articles, the ABDC will schedule news stories over the course of a few hours to ensure they are not dumped all at once and over-crowd the feed.

CHAPTER 40
LinkedIn

LinkedIn is the most business-oriented social media platform. It's for professional networking with colleagues, industry practitioners and others interested in your field. Hundreds of millions of people from all sectors of the economy share work, start conversations, join industry groups, find job opportunities, share experiences, engage with industry leaders and learn new skills.

> **"** *LinkedIn is useful simply because you can get out there to your industry audience.* **"**
>
> **STEVEN ROWLEY,** *CURTIN BUSINESS SCHOOL*

LinkedIn can be useful for academics as a semi-public space that allows the sharing of posts and articles with those in your network or with the wider LinkedIn community. LinkedIn posts and articles can consist of text, photos, videos and/or URLs, and may include hashtags to help reach a larger audience.

User profiles showcase specialities, work experience, education, voluntary work, interests and can also provide professional endorsements by other LinkedIn users. If kept up to date, a user's profile can be a digital CV that stays with you, not just with your current job.

'LinkedIn's useful for me just for checking out somebody's background and whether I need to call them Dr or not, stuff like that. Getting a sense of the experience they've had,' John Ross of *Times Higher Education* says.

Using LinkedIn can be an easy way to meet others teaching, working and researching in your field with tools like connecting and direct messaging to spark conversations.

> **"** *People sometimes approach me through direct messaging and that has opened up incredible opportunities.* **"**
>
> **ELIZABETH SHEEDY,** *MACQUARIE BUSINESS SCHOOL*

'It's a very polite forum…I very rarely see any rude or aggressive language on LinkedIn. I find LinkedIn a wonderful social media for supporting my research agenda,' Professor Sheedy says.

Frederik Anseel of UNSW Business School talks to a lot of people on LinkedIn who want to learn more and develop professionally.

He says a lot of people follow academics because they have access to trustworthy information and are not trying to sell anything. 'I try to put a story, or sort of an article, every week or twice a week. A lot of these things get picked up and they get a life on their own.'

Sometimes you get lucky

A *Business Think* interview of Professor Anseel discussing workplace changes and how they would accelerate smart cities was picked up globally by LinkedIn as one of the 21 Big Ideas for 2021.

'Suddenly there's a flood of requests, then people that want to talk to you and want to talk about that idea. Sometimes LinkedIn works like that,' Professor Anseel says.

Catherine Webber advises academics to always republish their media articles on LinkedIn. 'That's great for your profile. It's great for your institution.'

Beware the humble brag

For some, the proliferation of the 'humble brag' or low-level boasting on the platform can be a turn-off.

'I deleted the LinkedIn app off my phone because I believe that LinkedIn has become a very strange place with what I call the humble brag – *I'm honoured to have been honoured to have been asked to do this, honoured to have my paper published in whatever*,' Louise Grimmer of UTAS Business School says.

But for others, LinkedIn's appeal still lies in its supportive environment and ability to help users develop more focused content feeds. It's valuable for business leaders and others looking for relevant information, connections and networks and, partly because of that, aligns well with business school interests.

CHAPTER 41

Instagram

Instagram is an image-based social media platform where users can share permanent posts and temporary stories (content that only lasts for 24 hours). Owned by Facebook, the app is popular with Millennials and Gen Z who use it to keep up with friends and family and as a source of entertainment and knowledge-gathering. On the platform, users can post photos, stories and short and long-form videos.

For academics wanting to distribute content to a younger audience, Instagram's post carousel feature is a great way to share research as one post can incorporate text tiles, photos and video snippets. This posting style is widely used by organisations like *The Conversation*, The Australian Bureau of Statistics and *The Daily Aus* as it provides a quick and easy explainer for readers that can then be shared via followers' Stories to gain further reach. Instagram Stories are also a great way to engage with followers and institutions, and to keep them up to date with day-to-day activities.

CHAPTER 42

Facebook

Facebook is the world's largest social media platform used by billions worldwide.

Facebook is mainly used for personal reasons like connecting with friends and family, viewing news content and keeping up with common interest groups.

For academics, the ability to create private Facebook groups could be beneficial as they allow you to engage with other academics to whom you're connected and share research and ideas through multimedia posts in a private setting. Using Facebook can also be a useful way to engage with students through private class pages and events, and to stay up to date with what institutions are working on.

CHAPTER 43

YouTube

YouTube is a video-sharing platform used by billions of people around the world. On YouTube, creators can share long and short-form video, engage with the community through comments and find creators with similar interests.

For academics, making YouTube videos can be a great way to engage with students and others interested in your topic area, as the platform's flexible time-limit allows for detailed explanations and deep discussion. It also can help to grow your profile among YouTube's large learning community.

See the following channels for examples of effective educational explainers and case study videos: ABC News In Depth, Behind the News, Business Insider, Vox and SciShow.

CHAPTER 44

TikTok

TikTok is a short-form video sharing platform which was launched in 2018 as a place for bite-sized entertainment and educational content. TikTok's diverse audience of millions allows video creators to find a niche for their content and build a public profile.

If favoured by the TikTok algorithm, creators can grow their profile rapidly over the course of a few videos, because videos are shown on a person's *For You* page even though that person may not already follow the creator. For example, in only a few days, a friend of the author had more than 10 million views of one video and boosted her follower numbers from 1000 to over 100,000.

Learning is one of the TikTok's focus areas. Literary historian and PhD candidate, Esmé James (@esme.louisee) uses the platform to share interesting facts and research findings with her 1.7million+ followers. James' research area is *the aesthetics of sexual experience within 18th to 20th century literature... and how this can look at a more harmonious relationship for humans as a model.*

'One night I just decided to make this video on the earliest bedroom toy, posted it on TikTok, forgot that I'd done it, and came back two days later to that video having nearly 100,000 views and all of these followers wanting to hear more.'

James says the direct delivery to social media users stops information being stuck in the more insular academic community.

'Some of the research that we put our hearts and souls into generally will only reach an audience of 200, or maybe just at conferences and people who are already in this subject area. Social media changes that game,' she says.

Being tight on time sharpens your focus

The TikTok video time limit of three minutes (at the time of writing) has helped James learn to focus on what's most essential, which in turn affects how she teaches at The University of Melbourne.

It's a challenge to explain two years of research in 60 seconds but, James says, 'you learn over time how to take a very complex topic, choose the very few elements which are important, deliver your argument, deliver your evidence and then explain why it's important'.

'You can have a bigger conversation later, you can come to the comments section and make follow up videos later, but it does teach you to be concise, and that's very much helped me as a teacher.'

James has also found her TikTok presence helps her build wider academic connections and has changed how she works outside in-person meetings and conferences.

'I've been able to work with professors and researchers in Australia to make content for their upcoming courses. I've also been able to do videos for the State Library in Melbourne.

'I've met so many academics from around the world that I probably would never have met on such a similar topic. We now share research and we're looking towards joint publications. It's been life changing,' James says.

Initially a science experiment

Astrophysicist, science communicator and PhD candidate Kirsten Banks (@astrokirsten) says TikTok creation challenges her to communicate concisely and think creatively about how to make each video visually interesting.

Banks runs science outreach programs with schools and the public, but with her programs shut down during the pandemic, she still craved a way to talk about space. There was not a lot of science content on TikTok, so she decided to experiment.

Banks now has more than 315,000 followers. TikTok has provided professional and personal opportunities, which include creating content for NITV during National Science Week, making new friends in her field, working with brands, and being part of a TikTok-led program to create educational content.

Balancing TikTok and other academic commitments

Kirsten Banks and Esmé James have both developed strategies to balance regular content creation with more traditional academic commitments.

Banks posts a video a day but will sometimes record a batch of videos in one hit. She will then edit them during down times and have them ready to post ahead of time. It takes one or two hours to make a one-minute video, and longer if research is required. Banks allocates time to interact and comment on the TikTok app, but when her time is up she steps right away.

TikTok is big on collaboration between creators and between users and creators.

'They will sometimes comment or will send me messages, and sometimes they may be distantly related to the historical figure I was talking about and give me information that I've never seen on historical records or anything like that before. That not only shapes my research as an academic... it's that collaborative process as well. You never know who the real people are behind comments when you first see them, and they can sometimes be these incredible people,' James says.

Banks says creating content and interacting is time consuming, but worth the rewards. 'I don't think it's any more time consuming than things like Twitter. That has been such a big part of the academic community for so long, because I don't think any of us actually realise how long we're spending on Twitter. But I think you do have to be conscious in actually putting aside a time, so it doesn't impact your life.'

TIKTOK VIDEOS IN BUSINESS MANAGEMENT EDUCATION

Short TikTok videos with re-enactments of famous movie scenes have been created by Stuart Middleton of UQ Business School to help students understand key messages about business management.

'We have to get students interested and engaged; that's the main thing for me because it's so easy for them to fall through the cracks otherwise,' says Dr Middleton, an award-winning senior lecturer in strategy.

His efforts to teach in a novel way were brought about by COVID-19, but were also an attempt to capture the imaginations of a changing generation of students.

'The TikToks are 60-second re-enactments of famous movie scenes where I talk about strategic management. They were getting about 450 views and I think the students appreciate when they see somebody of my age making an effort around these things.

'I was hoping it would make me more approachable to the students if they saw me being a bit of a goose. Basically, I'm trying to keep it fun, that's the deal.

'I'm trying to mix things up but it's hard when students are in different time zones and different countries, facing all those big things in their lives that the world is dealing with at the moment,' he says.

His re-enactments include impersonations of famous characters such as Forrest Gump from the 1994 movie of the same name.

Dr Middleton's students include one from Myanmar who was about to be cut off the internet because of a military crackdown, one on a cattle station out west of Mackay and another who came to UQ for two weeks and was locked out in NSW with her family because of the pandemic.

'They've all got a lot going on and in a lot of ways are separated from what they've ever known, and I'm conscious of that in my teaching in trying to give students a sense of meaning and belonging.

'We really need to think about their greater wellbeing.'

Dr Middleton's methods to engage his students were recognised in 2021 with a Citation for Outstanding Contribution to Student Learning at UQ's Awards for Excellence in Teaching and Learning.

Dr Middleton was also awarded the Australia and New Zealand Academy of Management 'Innovative Management Educator of the Year' award for 2020.

Scan the landscape before stepping in

For academics wanting to begin creating TikToks, it's important to explore the app as a viewer and understand what makes something popular. Consider things like the style of content, tone of voice, background music options, trends and the visual look of the videos. From there you can create content, see what works for you and your audience, and develop your own voice.

Esmé James says its essential to be authentic as viewers know when someone is not being genuine.

When creating content and posting, James checks in with herself to ensure she is confident about the subject area and not trying to be someone else. 'I don't think it's very easy to put on a persona and try out different things. When you actually do want to build a community, you have to be yourself and your personality is just as important as your content.'

Big on collaboration and more casual

TikTok has developed into a more casual platform than LinkedIn or Instagram and promotes authentic content creation and community participation.

'[Sometimes when] I've posted a video, I will be dressed to the tens and my suit and my hair and everything, and I probably made this video a week ago and I'm posting it today. But people aren't surprised when they make a comment, and I will maybe make a video reply back to that comment to answer their questions. No one is going to raise an eyebrow if I'm now suddenly in my Oodie drinking my tea while I answer this question. People are accepting of the fact that we're human and we don't always have to be perfect figures,' James says.

Share your passion with the curious

James says there is a large community of curious people on TikTok 'who come on to that app to learn, whether it's different skills or different facts'.

> **❝** *If you have done research that you think will only reach a certain amount of people and maybe no one will be interested in it, they're sometimes the things that everyone wants to hear. If it's important to you, it's likely it's important to lots of people.* **❞**
>
> **ESMÉ JAMES,** *LITERARY HISTORIAN AND TIKTOK CREATOR*

Researchers are usually doing what they love. 'Bring that passion and that position of confidence to the app or whatever social media platform it is. Share the information or a fun fact that interests you. You don't have to jump straight in with making lessons and content, it can just be you talking about a fun fact you read in a book,' James says.

It's important to have fun with the app. 'There are ways for us to be creative without research, writing papers and visualising our data,' Banks says.

Researchers are usually doing what they love

8

Conclusion

CHAPTER 45

Is it ever a wrap?

- How do you plan to measure success?

- A measurement might be easy – but is it relevant?

- Constant engagement can result in useful feedback

- Keep gathering your evidence of media exposure

- Tips for measuring engagement and impact

At the start of this guide we discussed how communications are almost always works in progress. So too is evaluation of whether your efforts are hitting your marks.

It's obviously important to be clear initially on what you want to achieve, what success will look like and how to reach your goals.

But how will you measure your success in engaging and positively impacting the stakeholders you want to help or influence?

66 One of the dangers is people use what they can measure rather than what they need to measure. They can create a lot of noise that is interesting but not relevant, and actually confusing. 99

DIANE SHELTON, *FORMER CEO, FORETHOUGHT RESEARCH*

Measuring what's easy

Within communications we often use what is easiest to measure, including so-called 'vanity metrics' on social media, such as 'likes' or 'impressions'.

With back-end analytics we can see how many people are looking at parts of a website and how long they spend on a given page. Email newsletter distribution services can report who opens our newsletters and how many times they forward them. Media monitoring agencies can provide statistics to show that one story has reached a certain number of media consumers.

But say you are quoted in a media outlet that reaches one million people, or you have hundreds of thousands of followers on social media, or you are frequently posting content that inspires loads of reactions. Does this really give you the answers you need?

Who likes you? Who are your followers? Have you been able to cut through the noise and encourage people to apply your information in practical ways?

Can any of your work be attributed directly to a major shift in government policy, incremental industry changes or re-framing of public narratives?

Has media exposure of your work resulted in new industry or research partnerships? Has it attracted more students to your courses?

Or is it enough to accept that your work has made an unmeasurable contribution, along with the efforts of many others, to bring about social or economic change?

Constant engagement can equal frequent feedback

'When we talk about research impact, most people are able to say, *here is my research, I've published three articles based on this study.* To go and say *this is the way that the research changes society* is much harder. You need to actually get some feedback from people out there', Macquarie Business School's Debbie Haski-Leventhal says.

'But the more you are engaged with external stakeholders from business, industry, the not-for-profits, the government, the community and so on, the more likely you are to actually get this feedback that your research is making a difference.'

Food for thought

Sometimes you may just hope that a presentation will give the audience useful takeaways.

QUT Business School's Gary Mortimer says once, when he was with about 90 franchisees discussing innovative ways to engage customers, he remembers watching the franchisees – who had probably spent half a million dollars buying a franchise – taking notes.

'I had a coffee with them afterwards. I genuinely hope they walked away and put maybe one or two things I suggested into their business, to change the way they do business,' he says.

However, a more obvious impact stemmed from Professor Mortimer and colleagues talking to a major grocery chain about research on the importance of local food and why people care about locally grown and made products. After the discussion the chain appointed local purchasing managers in each state.

Continuously gathering evidence

UTAS Business School's Louise Grimmer is a believer in keeping and using the evidence of her work. She collates a file with PDFs of all stories, journal articles, book chapters and other articles.

'So, for example, I would say, *this year I've done over 60 interviews on COVID-19 across a range of different media or I have done 350 interviews in the last three years.*

'If you're going for promotion or you're applying for a grant or a committee or something, it's very powerful to be able to say *not only am I doing the research, the teaching service, but guess what? I can bring all of this stuff as well,*' Dr Grimmer says.

How public, or valuable to stakeholders, is your profile?

The following questions may be uncomfortable but are useful in ascertaining the effect of your profile on stakeholders:

- Have people heard of me?
- Are people familiar with what I have to offer?
- Would a stakeholder consider using me as an expert researcher, speaker or consultant?

And this question would be of great interest to your institution:

- How much does my public profile help to boost the number of students considering or signing up for courses?

Measuring dissemination, engagement and impact

In *Communicating Your Impact with Social Media*, Mollett et al. include this list of potential indicators.[68]

Dissemination: how many people are coming across your work:

- Reach of media content
- Listens or views of content on external sites
- Number of downloads or pageviews on project website
- Growth of followers on social media
- Retweets or shares from other influential social media accounts
- Mainstream media mentions (with estimated audience figures)
- Reposts on external sites
- Percentage of web traffic from social media
- Newsletter subscribers.

Engagement: online and in-person conversations stemming from your dissemination efforts:

- Range of content targeted at multiple target groups
- Likes, shares and comments on social media
- Mentions on social media from research beneficiaries
- Number of comments received
- Other blogs or websites linking to your content

- Time spent on page compared with other media
- Case studies of external partnerships
- Workshop attendance with diverse range of participants
- Sentiment analysis of social media related to research product.

Impact: demonstrable change resulting from either dissemination or public engagement:

- Reuse of data or software in another setting
- Invitations to speak at conferences and workshops
- Policy or decision makers mentioning research
- Industry partnerships or spin-offs based on research
- New collaborations emerging from research communication
- Effects on local/global community.

Clear progress on communicating well for change

There are innumerable ways to structure and implement evaluation of your communications. The main point here is to know what you want to do and be brave enough to assess progress objectively.

With that in hand, sharing research, knowledge, strong images and well-communicated stories will provide a much better chance of leading to positive cultural, environment, social and economic change.

68 Mollett, A, Brumley, C, Gilson C & Williams, S. 2017. *Communicating Your Research with Social Media: A Practical Guide to Using Blogs, Podcasts, Data Visualisations and Video*, Sage Publishing, London.

Index

About the ABDC

The Australian Business Deans Council (ABDC) represents 39 Australian university business schools, which teach more than one-quarter of the nation's university students and, prior to the pandemic disruptions, almost half of its international student graduates. It is known globally as the publisher of the widely used *ABDC Journal Quality List* that ranks peer-reviewed research journals in Australia and New Zealand.

For more information, go to abdc.edu.au, email comms@abdc.edu.au, follow us on Twitter @businessdeans or LinkedIn at https://www.linkedin.com/in/businessdeans.